Cakes for Occasions

Ann Pickard

Cakes for Occasions

25 special cakes for every celebration

GUILD OF MASTER
CRAFTSMAN PUBLICATIONS

First published 2011 by
Guild of Master Craftsman Publications Ltd
Castle Place, 166 High Street, Lewes,
East Sussex BN7 1XU

ISBN 978 1 86108 826 0

Publisher Jonathan Bailey
Production Manager Jim Bulley
Managing Editor Gerrie Purcell
Senior Project Editor Dominique Page
Editor Kathy Steer
Managing Art Editor Gilda Pacitti
Design Chloë Alexander

Set in Amperzand, Avenir, Chapparal and
My type of font
Colour origination by GMC Reprographics
Printed and bound by C&C Offset in China

Dedication
With love to Markie Jazzie and Gemma.
With thanks to Dave Pinnock, Nick Sparks, Jill Barker,
Carole Erison, Celine Ollivier and Ruth O'Connell.

Contents

CAKE BASICS

BIRTHDAY CAKES

CHILDREN'S CAKES

BABY CAKES

THIS CAKE IS IDEAL FOR A CHRISTENING. MAKE SURE
THAT YOU ALLOW ENOUGH TIME FOR THE PASTILLAGE PIECES
AND SUGARPASTE BLOCK TO DRY.

Miniature Crib

You will need

- 5in (12.5cm) pink covered cake on 5in (12.5cm) thin card
- 8in (20cm) light pink covered cake on a 12in (30cm) round cake drum
- 14in (35cm) white covered cake drum
- 6½oz (180g) white pastillage
- 2½oz (60g) pale pink pastillage
- 1oz (30g) dark pink pastillage
- 1oz (30g) skin-coloured sugarpaste
- 4oz (115g) white sugarpaste

- 1oz (30g) pale pink sugarpaste
- 2½oz (60g) royal icing
- Liquorice black paste colour
- Cocktail stick or toothpick
- 3–4in (8–10cm) oval plaque cutter
- Large, medium and small heart cutters
- 3ft (1m) of ⅝in (15mm) dark pink ribbon
- 3ft (1m) of ¼in (5mm) white ribbon

Continued on page 13

10

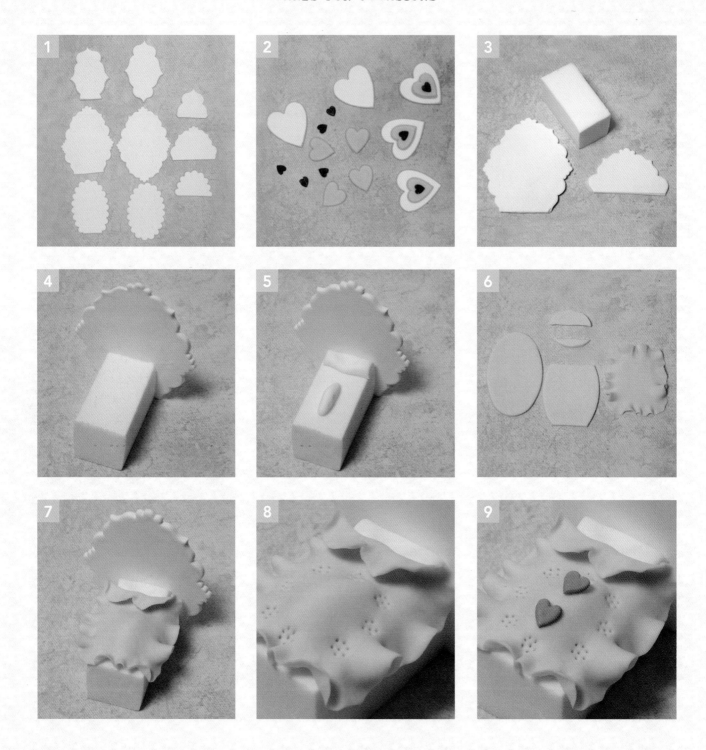

Continued from page 10
- Paper piping bags
- No. 1 piping tube or nozzle
- Bulbous cone modelling tool
- Guide to Sizes chart (see page 165)

ADVANCE PREPARATION

Cut all the pastillage pieces and the sugarpaste block 48 hours before assembling your cake (see steps one to three).

1 Using the white pastillage, cut two oval shapes with any small plaque cutter (a variety are available, as shown). Take a small slice off the end of one of the plaques. Cut the other in half.

2 Roll out the white pastillage ⅛in (2mm) thick on a work surface dusted with icing sugar and cut 22 large hearts, roll out and cut 26 small dark pink hearts, then roll out and cut 24 medium light pink hearts. Allow to dry then stick 22 together in threes. Make two double hearts using the two smaller sizes. Use royal icing to stick them together.

3 Cut a block of sugarpaste 3 x 1in (7.5 x 2.5cm) and 1¼in (3cm) high. Allow to dry for 48 hours. This will be the base of your crib. The back piece will be the large plaque and the front piece will be one of the halves.

CRIB

4 When all the pieces are completely dry, stick the back to the crib with a little royal icing to secure. The cut edge will be at the bottom of the crib.

5 Form two little balls of icing, both size G, and roll each one into a tapered sausage shape 1in (2.5cm) long. Stick one down the middle of the crib base, place the other one at the top for a pillow and make a dent in the middle of the pillow.

6 Roll out the pale pink sugarpaste and cut a 3in (7.5cm) oval shape. Cut the top and bottom off and frill all around the edge (see 'How to frill sugarpaste', page 164).

7 Brush a little apricot purée or sugar glue on to the body and base of the crib. Place your blanket on top and turn down the top edge. Make sure the end of the blanket doesn't go over the edge of the crib.

8 Using a cocktail stick, mark little circular flower shapes around the outer edge of the blanket; leave the space in the centre of the blanket unmarked.

9 Take two of your dark pink small hearts and stick them to the top of your blanket with a little piped royal icing.

Guide to sizes	
Head	**F**
Nose	**K**

BABY

10 Form the baby's head shape from a ball, size F, using skin-coloured sugarpaste. Mark the ears with the end of the modelling tool; make a hole for the face and insert the nose, size K. Mark the eyes (see 'Eyes', page 166) with black paste colour. With the gentlest touch, add two tiny dots to create the eyebrows.

11 Place the baby's head into the crib; stick it to your pillow with royal icing. At this stage, if you wish, the baby can have hair piped on (see 'Piping hair', page 169).

FINISHING OFF

12 Stick one of your three-layered hearts at the top of the back of the crib; use a lot of royal icing to secure. Stick a double heart to the middle of the crib front.

13 Place a No. 1 piping tube into a paper piping bag. Half-fill with royal icing and pipe little dots in flower shapes on the crib back and front. Pipe five dots in a circle and one in the middle.

14 Attach two pieces of ribbon around the top tier of your cake and secure with a little piped royal icing. Ensure that the joins are at the back of the cake.

15 Pipe two balls of icing on the back of the heart on the two top curves and stick three-layered hearts to the side of the cake, sloping outwards. Push the point at the bottom of the heart gently into the icing on the board; this will help hold them in place. Stick your finished two-tier cake onto the iced 14in (35cm) cake drum.

ALTERNATIVES

16 Here are some examples of cribs that have been made using different plaque cutters and with different coloured covers. They all look equally effective.

IF YOU NEED A LARGER CAKE, MAKE A TWO-TIER CAKE AND HAVE THIS DELIGHTFUL BED AS YOUR TOP TIER. YOU CAN ALSO PAINT THE BABY'S NAME ON THE BACK OF THE BED, IF YOU WISH.

Baby's First Bed

You will need

- 6in (15cm) square cake covered in blue sugarpaste on a 10in (25cm) square white covered board
- 3½oz (100g) blue sugarpaste
- 2½oz (60g) light brown sugarpaste
- ½oz (15g) dark brown sugarpaste
- 2½oz (60g) skin-coloured sugarpaste
- 8oz (225g) white sugarpaste
- 6oz (175g) pastillage
- Liquorice black paste colour
- 2½oz (60g) royal icing
- Large round 5–6½in (12.5–17cm) plaque cutter
- Paintbrush
- Cocktail stick or toothpick
- Bulbous cone modelling tool
- Paper piping bags
- Guide to Sizes chart (see page 165)

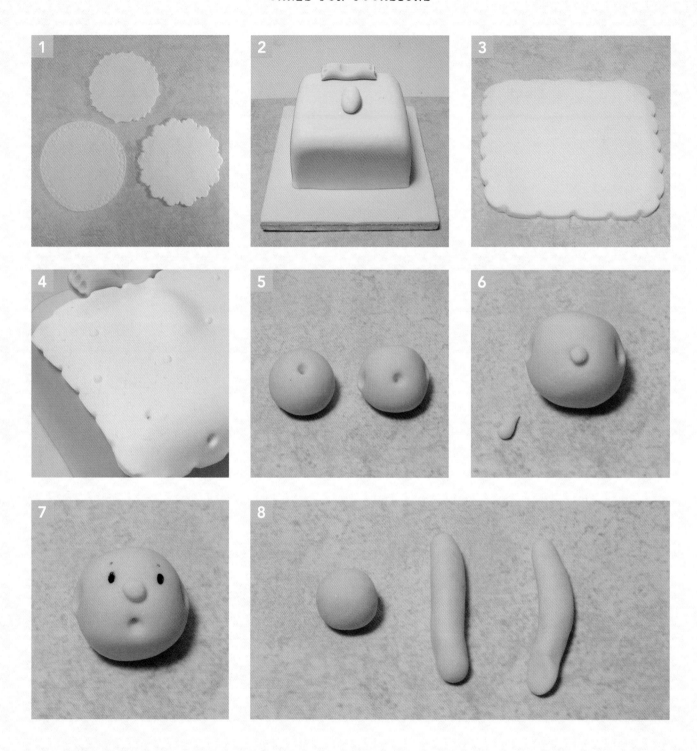

BED

1 Use any large round plaque cutter to cut out the back of your bed. Roll out the pastillage ⅛–⅙in (3–4mm) thick on a work surface well dusted with icing sugar and cut firmly. Allow to dry for 48 hours on the back of a cake board dusted with icing sugar. Turn over halfway through drying.

TIP: *If you don't have a plaque cutter you could cut around a board or a plate to create a plain back to your bed.*

2 Form a 4in (10cm) sausage of blue sugarpaste. Cut each end sloping downwards and impress each end of the pillow three times with the rounded end of the modelling tool, then press a dent in the middle of the pillow with your thumb. From a ball size C, make a flattened oval shape for the body.

3 Cut a 7in (18cm) square shape with rounded corners from the white sugarpaste for the top blanket. Using the pointed end of the modelling tool, push little indents all around the edge at 1in (2.5cm) intervals. Spread a little apricot purée or water on your cake top and body and stick the cover in place.

4 Using the pointed end of the tool again, make widely spaced holes in the top of the blanket. Roll some tiny white balls and place them in the holes, sticking them with a little-brushed on water or sugar glue.

BABY

5 Start to form the baby's head – you will need a ball, size C, in skin-coloured sugarpaste. Flatten the back of the head and make a hole in the centre of the face ready for the nose with the end of the modelling tool. Make an indent each side of the head for the ears.

6 Form a tiny, skin-coloured nose, size I, and shape it into a teardrop. Carefully insert into the hole in the face. Press in gently but do not squash flat.

7 Use a cocktail stick dipped into black paste colour to mark the eyes (see 'Eyes' page 166). Mark little oval-shaped eyes and then, with the gentlest touch, add two tiny dots for the eyebrows. Scratch on some little lines at the top of the baby's head to represent fine hair.

8 Form one little arm from skin-coloured sugarpaste, size E. Roll it into a sausage 2in (5cm) long, flatten the end for the palm and slightly pinch in the wrist. Repeat for the second arm.

Guide to sizes	
BABY	
Head	*C*
Nose	*I*
Arms	*2 x E*
Body (under blanket)	*C*
DOG	
Body	*C*
Legs	*4 x F*
Head	*E*
Tail	*G*
Ears	*2 x G*
Nose	*H*

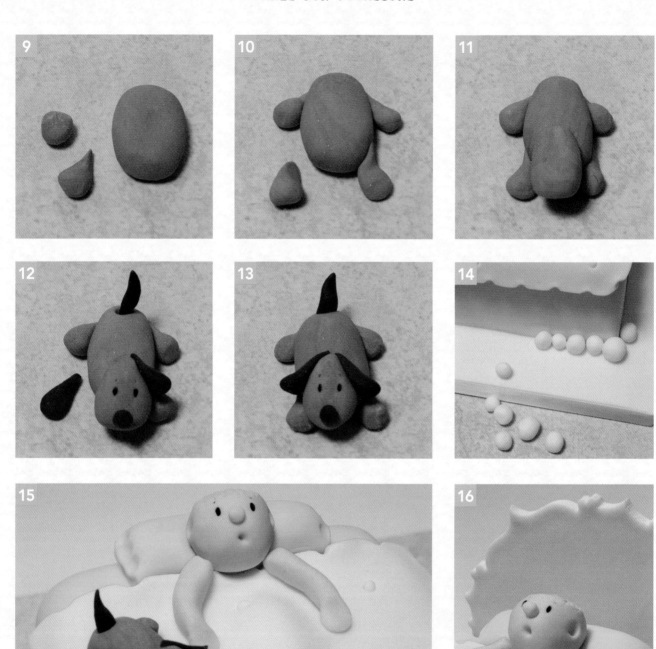

DOG

9 The body is a ball of light brown sugarpaste, size C, formed into a short sausage shape 1½in (4cm) long. Start to form the first leg, size F, into a teardrop.

10 Stick the first leg to the body, using sugar glue if necessary. The pointed end is attached to the body and the fatter end is at the front. Make three more legs and attach.

TIP: *If you make each leg and attach immediately it should stick by itself. Don't prepare them all in advance and then try to attach to the body as they will dry out.*

11 When all the legs are firmly in place, make a dent with your finger at the front end of the dog ready to stick your head on. Form the head, size E, into a cone shape and stick it in place with the pointed end at the top.

12 Form a dark brown ear, size G, into a long cone shape, flatten it and stick it to the side of the head. Repeat for the other ear. Make a hole for the tail and the nose and push in a cone shape for the nose, size H, and a pointy sausage shape for the tail, size G. When all the sections of the dog are made, mark the eyes with black paste colour (see 'Eyes', page 166). With the gentlest touch, add two tiny dots for the eyebrows.

13 Your dog is now complete, so for a variation why not make him fluffy? Ruffle the surface of his body with a cocktail stick (see the teddy bear on 'Alphabet Bear', page 138).

FINISHING OFF

14 Form lots of little white balls of sugarpaste in various sizes and stick them all around the base of your cake. You can use sugar glue to stick them if they are soft or piped royal icing if they are hard.

15 Place the baby's head on to the pillow and add the arms over the cover. Arrange the dog on the blanket by one of the hands.

16 Carefully remove your large plaque from the drying board. Brush off any excess icing sugar and stick firmly to the back of the bed with royal icing.

THIS IS A DELIGHTFUL, PRETTY CAKE. WHY NOT ADD ANOTHER MOUSE TO MAKE AN ENGAGEMENT CAKE? MAKE SURE THE FLOWERS, FLOWERBUDS AND GRASS ARE GIVEN TIME TO DRY.

Little Mouse

You will need

- 7 x 5in (18 x 12.5cm) oval cake on an 11in (28cm) round drum covered in pale green sugarpaste. Polish your cake surface with white satin shimmer
- 2½oz (60g) royal icing
- 1oz (30g) bright pink pastillage
- 1oz (30g) pale green pastillage
- 4oz (115g) pale grey sugarpaste
- ½oz (15g) pale pink sugarpaste
- Liquorice black paste colour
- 22-gauge white flower wires

- Disco white hologram edible glitter
- Small daisy cutter
- 3in (7.5cm) oval cutter
- White and green ribbon
- Bulbous cone modelling tool
- Raw spaghetti
- Paper piping bags
- Small posy pick
- Green ribbon
- Guide to Sizes chart (see page 165)

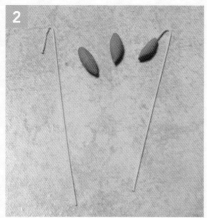

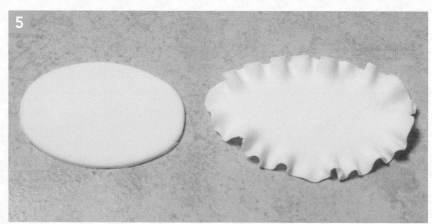

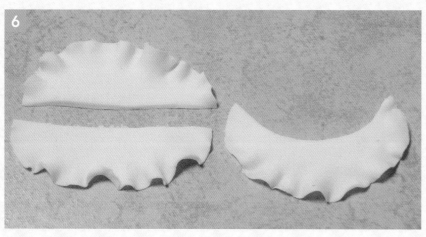

ADVANCE PREPARATION

Prepare steps one to four 24 hours before you require them to allow them to dry.

1 Roll out the pink pastillage to a ⅛in (3mm) thickness. Using a small daisy cutter, cut five or six flower shapes. Pinch each petal firmly to thin it and curve them all slightly upwards. Push a 22-gauge flower wire dipped into sugar glue up into the flower. Allow to dry.

2 Form four or five little bud shapes from the pink pastillage. Bend the wires over at the end. Paint a little sugar glue on the bent end and push into the buds.

3 Now roll out the pale green pastillage to a ⅛in (2mm) thickness. Cut some long sections of grass and some individual blades too. Allow everything to dry on a board dusted with icing sugar.

4 When the flowers are dry, pipe a large ball of white royal icing in the centre. Allow it to slightly set, then squash it flat and sprinkle with glitter.

FRILLS

5 Cut out a 3in (7.5cm) plain oval shape and frill all around the edge with the modelling tool (see 'How to frill sugarpaste', page 164). You will need to cut three to go around your cake but do one at a time and stick it on before making the next.

6 Cut the frilled oval in half lengthways and curve it slightly so that it will fit around the side of the cake.

7 Place a band of ribbon around your cake, then stick each frill in place using a little royal icing. Stick the first one on centre front and then work away from it to each side. If the cake is larger, you may need more frills or stretch them a little to make them longer. Make one more complete frill for the top of the cake.

Guide to sizes	
Body	*B*
Legs and arms	*4 x F*
Head	*D*
Ears	*2 x F*
Pink inner ear	*2 x G*
Tail	*E*

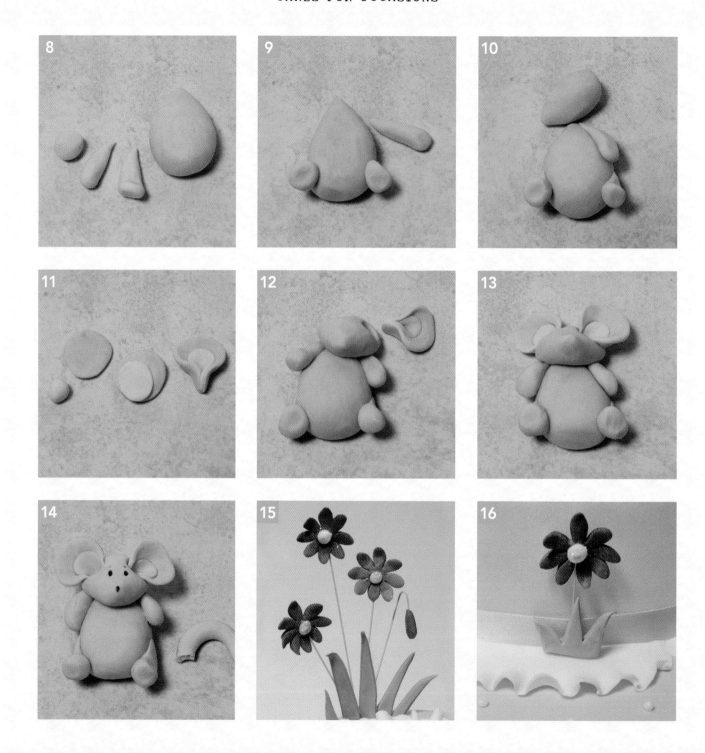

MOUSE

8 Form the mouse body from a ball, size B, in pale grey sugarpaste. Shape into a cone and sit his bottom firmly on the work surface to make a flat base. Shape two legs, size F, into pointy cone shapes and stick one each side of the body using sugar glue. Pinch and bend the soles of the feet upwards.

9 Shape two arms, size F, and using a little brushed-on sugar glue, stick to the sides of the body; the tops of the two arms want to meet at his neck.

10 The head is a pointed cone shape formed from a ball, size D. Push a piece of raw spaghetti down into the body and break it off ½in (1cm) above the neck. Place the head down on to the spaghetti.

11 Squash a pink ball, size G, and a grey ball, size F, flat. Place the pink one on top of the other and press down well. Pinch to form the ear shape and repeat for the second ear.

12 Make two very large holes with the pointed end of the modelling tool. The holes need to be pointing in at two o'clock and eleven o'clock if you imagine the head is a clock face.

13 Place the prepared ears into the holes; if they fall out then make the hole bigger until they rest in place by themselves. To secure them, push the modelling tool into the middle of each ear and twist, then remove it. Mark the eyes and nose (see 'Eyes', page 166) with black paste colour. With the gentlest touch, add two tiny dots for the eyebrows.

14 Now form a ball of grey sugarpaste, size E, into a long tail trailing to a point at one end. When you put your mouse on the cake, tuck the fat end of the tail under his bottom and drape the other end over the edge of the cake.

FINISHING OFF

15 Push the end of the flower and bud wires into a posy pick and push the posy pick into the top of the cake behind the top frill. Place the grass piece in front, pushing its base into the top of the cake, or stick with a little royal icing.

16 To secure your flowers around the side of the cake, tuck the wire behind the ribbon and stick the back of the flower to the cake side. Stick some grass with royal icing too. Pipe some royal icing balls on to the board and sprinkle with glitter when they are still wet. Finish with a green ribbon around the cake drum.

SEASONAL CAKES

THIS SPARKLY WINTER CAKE IS SO QUICK TO MAKE AND LOOKS REALLY EFFECTIVE, BUT DO REMEMBER TO PREPARE YOUR SNOWFLAKES IN ADVANCE SO THEY CAN DRY.

Glittery Snowflakes

You will need

- 5in (12.5cm) round cake 3in (7.5cm) high covered in blue sugarpaste
- 10in (25cm) round cake board
- 20in (0.5m) wide tearing ribbon
- 4½oz (120g) pastillage
- 2lb 4oz (1kg) royal icing
- White satin shimmer

- Paper piping bags
- No. 1.5 piping tube
- Small palette knife
- Set of large snowflake cutters
- Edible white glitter
- Small flat makeup sponge
- White ribbon

ADVANCE PREPARATION

Prepare step one 48 hours before you require the cake to allow the snowflakes to dry.

1 Roll the pastillage out to a thickness of ⅛in (4mm) and cut out the largest snowflake shapes; immediately cut out the centre with a small cutter. Transfer to a board lightly dusted with icing sugar to dry. Roll out the pastillage again a little thinner and cut out a selection of smaller snowflake shapes. Place on drying board.

TIP: *Cut out a few extras of the largest size to allow for any breakages.*

TIP: *Turn your snowflakes over halfway through the drying process.*

SNOWFLAKES

2 When your snowflakes are completely hard, spread them thinly with royal icing. Spike up the icing and sprinkle generously with edible glitter – the glitter will stick to the wet royal icing.

SNOW

3 Polish your cake surface with white satin shimmer on a flat makeup sponge. Wrap the strip of wide tearing ribbon around the top of the cake leaving 1½in (4cm) of cake showing below. Secure it tightly at the back with a round-headed pin. Begin to spread royal icing onto the cake board and up the side of the cake.

4 Continue to add royal icing until all the side of the cake below the ribbon is covered and all of the board too. Using a fork or small palette knife, ruffle up the icing; if you expose any of the cake or board while you are doing this just add some more icing to cover the hole.

5 Remove the pin and store safely. Now very carefully lift the piece of ribbon up and away; this will leave you with a sharp line around the cake where the white icing stops and the blue begins.

6 Place a No. 1.5 piping tube into a small paper piping bag. Fill a third of the bag with royal icing and pipe a selection of different-sized balls all over the cake to represent tiny snowballs.

FINISHING OFF

7 Very carefully push one of your large snowflakes into the top surface of the cake and press down until it is firmly in place. Arrange a few smaller snowflakes in the royal icing snow at the front.

8 Place another large snowflake at the front of the cake with its points pushed into the royal icing and arrange some others around the sides and back of the cake. Finally, neatly hide the edges of the cake board by sticking on a strip of ribbon.

AN EASY AND FESTIVE CAKE TO DECORATE: CHILDREN WILL
LOVE TO HELP SQUASHING THE SUGARPASTE BALLS ON THE CAKE,
CUTTING THE LEAVES AND MAKING THE BERRIES.

Figgy Pudding

You will need

- 2 x 6in (15cm) round chocolate sponges, each 2¾in (7cm) deep
- Chocolate filling cream
- 10in (25cm) round cake drum
- 2lb 12oz (1.2kg) chocolate sugarpaste
- 1lb (450g) red sugarpaste
- 1oz (30g) black sugarpaste
- 1oz (30g) white sugarpaste
- 8oz (225g) dark yellow royal icing
- Holly leaf cutter
- Plunger cutter (optional)
- Paper piping bags
- Paintbrush
- Red ribbon

1 Cut both your cakes in half and sandwich with chocolate filling cream, then place them on top of each other with a thin layer of cream in between. Shave away the top edges until you have created a ball shape. Spread thinly all over with chocolate cream.

TIP: *If your cake is crumbly, place it in the freezer after sandwiching together and leave for 30 minutes, then carve your shape.*

2 Roll out the chocolate brown sugarpaste on a work surface dusted with icing sugar to a circle about 12in (30cm) in diameter. Carefully lift the icing on to the cake and smooth all over with the palms of your hands until it is stuck on to the cake. Use two plastic smoothers for the best result (see 'Covering a cake', page 160).

DRIED FRUIT

3 Roll out a strip of red sugarpaste and cover the silver cake drum – several strips can be joined together; smooth over any joins to blend the lines in. Mix a little brown sugarpaste with some white sugarpaste and start to squash on the little balls of icing in light and dark brown. Brush on a dot of apricot purée or water to hold them in place.

4 Continue to add more and more squashed balls of sugarpaste, overlap some of them and make sure they are different sizes. Add lots of little black ones too and a few red ones to represent cherries. Make a few extras and stick them on the board but do not squash these ones.

LEAVES

5 Roll out the small piece of dark green sugarpaste to a ⅛in (3mm) thickness. You need three holly leaves, but cut a few spares in case you break some. Either use a plunger cutter that impresses the veining for you or mark a few lines on afterwards with a knife. Pinch the ends of the leaves upwards so they do not dry completely flat.

CUSTARD

6 Place the dark yellow royal icing in a small bowl and add a few drops of water to make the consistency slightly runny – do not add too much water as you don't want the 'custard' to drip all the way down the side of the cake. Half-fill a large paper piping bag, cut a ½in (1cm) hole in the end and pipe the shape shown in the photograph.

FINISHING OFF

7 Form a few large holly berries from red sugarpaste and place five or six on the very top of your cake while the 'custard' is still wet. Arrange three holly leaves around the berries.

8 With any remaining yellow royal icing, pipe some additional pools of 'custard' on to the iced board. Cut a length of ribbon and stick it around your board edge to complete your design.

PERFECT FOR A HALLOWEEN PARTY, YOUR GUESTS WILL SIMPLY LOVE THIS CAKE SHAPED INTO A PUMPKIN AND DECORATED WITH A BLACK CAT AND SCARY SPIDERS.

Halloween Pumpkin

You will need

- 5in (12.5cm) round cake 5in (12.5cm) high cut into a ball shape covered in 1lb 8oz (675g) orange sugarpaste
- 12in (30cm) round cake drum
- 1lb (450g) pale grey sugarpaste
- 8oz (225g) black sugarpaste
- 1oz (30g) green sugarpaste
- 1oz (30g) beige sugarpaste
- 1oz (30g) brown sugarpaste
- Small ball of white sugarpaste

- Small ball of red sugarpaste
- Black royal icing
- Paintbrush
- Cocktail stick or toothpick
- Paper piping bags
- No. 1 piping tube
- Bulbous cone modelling tool
- Raw spaghetti
- Cocktail stick or toothpick
- Guide to Sizes chart (see page 165)

FOR A VALENTINE TREAT, MAKE THIS CAKE FOR SOMEONE
YOU LOVE. YOU COULD USE SILVER DRAGEE BALLS
AND SILVER BEADING INSTEAD OF THE GOLD.

Valentine Heart

You will need

- 8in (20cm) heart-shaped cake covered in chocolate brown sugarpaste on a 12in (30cm) round cake drum covered in red sugarpaste
- 10oz (280g) cream sugarpaste
- 6½oz (180g) red sugarpaste
- 4oz (115g) chocolate brown sugarpaste
- Large closed curve crimper

- ⅙in (4mm) gold dragees (balls)
- Gold beading
- Paintbrush
- Chocolate-coloured royal icing
- Paper piping bags
- All sizes heart cutters

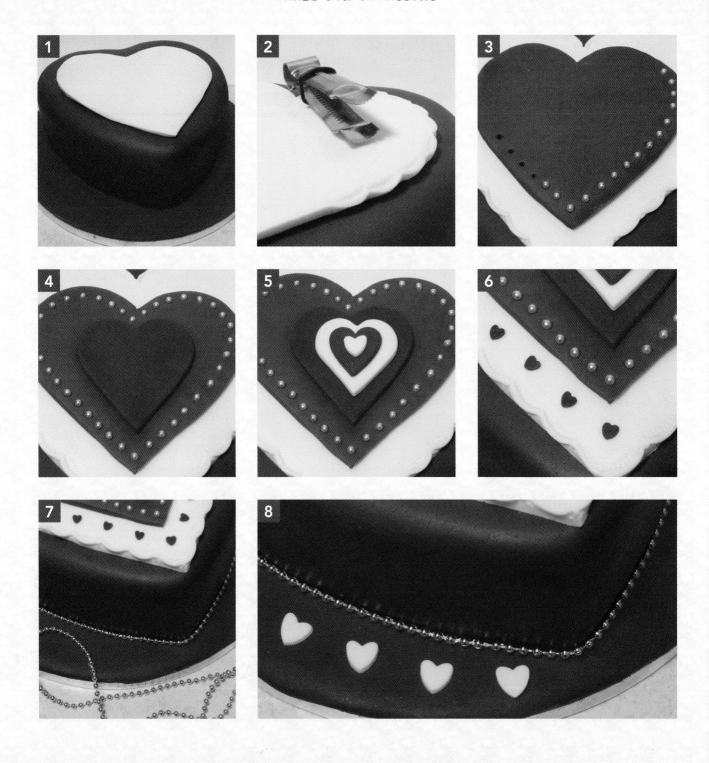

HEART SHAPES

1 Cut out a large 7in (18cm) heart shape ⅛in (4mm) thick in cream sugarpaste; stick to the top of your cake with apricot purée.

2 Using a pair of large closed curve crimpers, crimp all the way around the outside of your cream heart.

3 Roll out and cut a 5in (12.5cm) red heart shape. Stick this to the centre of your cream heart. Immediately push little gold dragees into the icing in a heart shape.

4 Cut out a 3¼in (8cm) chocolate sugarpaste heart shape and stick this to the centre of your red heart.

5 Roll out some red and cream sugarpaste, then cut out the three hearts and stick to each other on the top of your cake, using apricot purée or sugar glue to secure.

6 Cut out approximately 20 small chocolate hearts and stick them around the large cream heart. Make sure they are evenly spaced and stick them with sugar glue.

7 Add a length of gold beading all around the bottom of the cake, sticking with a little chocolate royal icing.

FINISHING OFF

8 Finish your design by sticking cream hearts all around your covered cake drum at evenly spaced intervals.

THIS DUCK POND IS A SUPER SEASONAL CAKE OR WOULD MAKE A LOVELY BIRTHDAY CAKE FOR A TODDLER. YOU CAN MAKE YOUR FAMILY OF DUCKS AS FAR IN ADVANCE AS YOU WISH.

Duck Pond

You will need

- 6in (15cm) cake covered in blue sugarpaste on a 10in (25cm) cake drum covered in green sugarpaste
- 6½oz (180g) yellow sugarpaste
- 8oz (225g) marbled grey sugarpaste
- ½oz (15g) red sugarpaste

- 4oz (115g) green royal icing
- 2 tablespoons piping gel
- Liquorice black paste colour
- Cocktail stick or toothpick
- Guide to Sizes chart (see page 165)

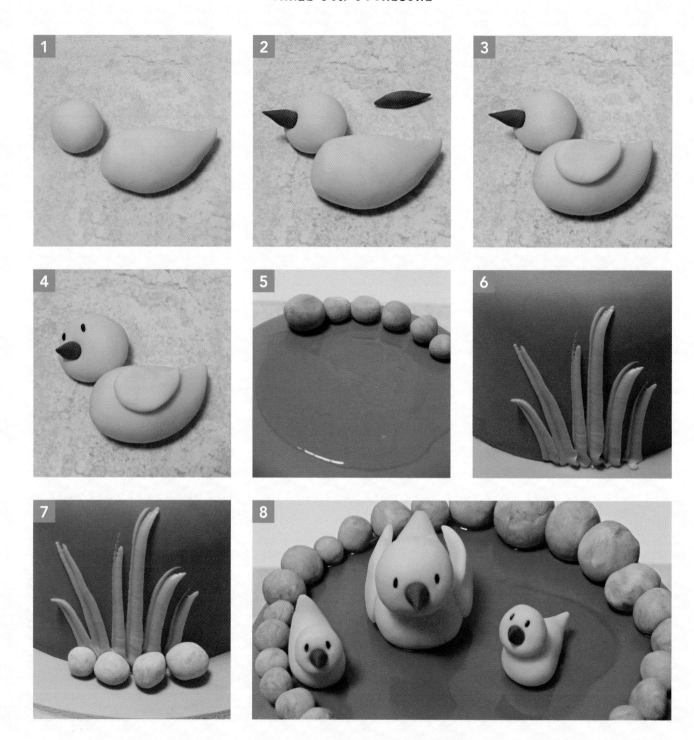

DUCKS

1 Form a ball of icing for the head and check it on the Guide to Sizes chart (see page 165) to make sure it fits on the correct circle. Shape the body into a long cone shape and bend the point upwards.

2 Stick the head firmly down on to the rounded end of the body and press down to secure. Make a hole with the pointed end of the modelling tool in the middle of the face. Form the red beak from the red sugarpaste into a long diamond shape and push half of the beak into the hole in the face.

3 Shape each of your two little wings into a cone shape. Squash each one flat and press one to each side of the body for the little wings – there is no need to make wings for the baby ducks as they are very small and fiddly.

4 Finish your large ducks with two oval-shaped black eyes marked with a cocktail stick and black paste colour (see 'Eyes', page 166). Now make some baby ducks following steps 1 and 2 using sizes as per Guide to Sizes chart on page 165.

POND

5 Using your grey sugarpaste, form lots of little pebbles, all different sizes, to go around the pond. Place a few on the cake to check their size then spread on the piping gel in a circle and stick the pebbles all around the edge of the circle.

6 Half-fill your piping bag with green royal icing. Squeeze it all the way to the end, flatten the end and cut the bag as shown on page 168 for 'Piping grass'. Pipe up the side with long strokes, pulling away at the end to form a point.

7 Make some extra pebbles and arrange them around the board at the base of the grass. Add extra little clumps of grass all around the base of the cake too.

FINISHING OFF

8 Arrange your little family of ducks into the pond on top of the cake. A few little ducks will look great around the board too.

Guide to sizes	
LARGE DUCK	
Body	*B*
Head	*D*
Wings	*2 x F*
Beak	*small G*
SMALL DUCK	
Body	*E*
Head	*F*
Wings	
Beak	*small H*
Ears	*2 x G*
Nose	*H*

WEDDING
CAKES

THIS COMBINATION OF CREAM ICING, CHOCOLATE CAKE AND
CHOCOLATE HEARTS IS IRRESISTIBLE. MAKE THE HEARTS
IN ADVANCE, AS THEY NEED TO DRY.

Chocolate Ruffles

You will need

- 8in (20cm) x 4in (10cm) high chocolate cake covered in thin chocolate brown sugarpaste on a 12in (30cm) cake drum
- 2lb 12oz (1.2kg) Belgian white chocolate paste or cream sugarpaste mixed with 3oz (90g) pastillage
- 2½oz (60g) dark chocolate colour pastillage
- 2½oz (60g) cream pastillage

- Royal icing
- A little dark brown and cream royal icing
- Pearl lustre spray
- Set of curving funky heart cutters
- Paper piping bags
- No. 1 piping tubes

THIS IS QUITE A MODERN DESIGN, BUT FOR A MORE TRADITIONAL LOOK THE TOP ARRANGEMENT COULD BE CHANGED TO A POSY OF FRESH OR SILK FLOWERS.

White Sparkles

You will need

- 5in (12.5cm) round white sugarpasted cake on a 4in (10cm) thin card
- 9in (23cm) round white sugarpasted cake on an 11in (28cm) round cake drum.
- 14in (35cm) drum covered in 1lb 8oz (675g) white sugarpaste
- 8in (20cm) round cake drum
- 4oz (115g) white pastillage
- 3¼in (8cm) pot or container with straight sides

- Lots of paper piping bags
- 10 x 22-gauge white wires
- Medium posy pick, plus small piece white sugarpaste
- No. 4, 3, 2, 1.5 piping tubes or nozzles
- 1lb (450g) royal icing
- 2 pots disco white hologram edible glitter
- 1 pot white satin shimmer
- Flat makeup sponge
- Sparkly white ribbon
- Plastic dowelling (optional)

ADVANCE PREPARATION

Prepare steps one and two at least 48 hours before finishing the cake.

1 Cut 10 wires into two pieces, some of them long and others shorter. Hook the end of each wire into a tiny loop, dip into a little sugar glue, and push on to a round ball of pastillage. Twist it so that it stays in place. Stick the end of the wire into a piece of polystyrene and allow to dry. After 48 hours, brush each one with sugar glue and dip into disco white hologram glitter. Allow to dry.

2 You will need a pot about 3¼in (8cm) in diameter with straight sides. Dust its sides with icing sugar. Roll out a strip of pastillage ⅛–¼in (4–5mm) thick and cut the crown shape using the template on page 173. Immediately wrap this around the pot, sticking the overlap with a little sugar glue; smooth down the overlapping join. Leave in a warm dry place for at least 48 hours. After 24 hours, remove the pot carefully to allow the inside to dry too.

BALLS

3 Stick the top tier on the centre of the bottom tier – if the lower tier is sponge, dowel it first (see 'Dowelling a cake', page 163).

Secure with a little royal icing. Using a flat makeup sponge, polish your cake surfaces all over with white satin shimmer; also polish the iced board. Using a No. 4 piping tube, pipe the first row of balls at the base of the cake.

TIP: *Always allow the surface of your cake to dry for 24 hours before polishing on shimmer.*

TIP: *Only pipe a 3–4in (7–10cm) section at a time, as you want it to be still wet when you sprinkle the glitter on – so that it sticks and stays in place.*

4 Using a No. 2 piping tube fitted into a small paper piping bag, pipe your top row of curving balls; either try freehand or scratch the surface of the cake beforehand to give you a guide to follow.

5 Place a No. 3 piping tube into a small paper piping bag. Half-fill with royal icing and fill in the space in between. Keep the balls close together and try to avoid any gaps in the icing. If there are any, just fill in with a little piped ball.

6 Finally, using a No. 1.5 piping tube or nozzle, pipe a small neat row of balls all along the top edge of the curves. At the top of

each point, pipe three graduated dots, decreasing in size as they go upwards. As you finish each small section sprinkle with glitter – it should stick in place and be really sparkly. Repeat all the stages for the next section of the cake, sprinkle that then continue.

CROWN

7 Place a little sausage of sugarpaste in the posy pick and push in the wires. Start with the taller wires with larger balls in the centre and the others all around. Don't worry if it looks messy as the wires can be moved when it is in place. Finish and allow your crown to dry (see Step 8) before pushing the posy pick into the middle of it.

8 To finish the crown, place it on top of the cake and secure with a little piped royal icing around the inner edge. Repeat the piping steps three to four on the sides of your crown, then sprinkle generously with glitter. Push the posy pick with the glitter balls into the centre of the cake until it isn't visible. Move the wires if necessary.

TIP: *The cake is displayed on the large iced board with the 8in (20cm) drum on top hidden underneath the wedding cake.*

THIS IS ONE OF THE EASIEST CAKES IN THE BOOK TO DECORATE YET IT LOOKS VERY EFFECTIVE. IT IS ALSO PERFECTLY SUITED TO FIT ANY OCCASION.

Funky Flowers

You will need

- 9in (23cm) round cake covered in pale green sugarpaste on a 12in (30cm) round cake drum
- 5in (12.5cm) round cake covered in pale green sugarpaste on a 5in (12.5cm) thin card
- 14in (35cm) drum covered in white sugarpaste
- 2½oz (60g) white sugarpaste
- 3oz (90g) white sugarpaste mixed with ½oz (15g) pastillage

- Royal icing
- Paper piping bags
- White satin shimmer
- Pearl lustre spray
- Large set of funky flower cutters
- Small set of funky flower cutters
- Piece of white paper
- Kitchen roll inner tube

Continued on page 65

THIS IS A FABULOUS MODERN WEDDING OR CELEBRATION CAKE;
JUST CHANGE THE COLOURS TO CREATE A DIFFERENT LOOK.
YOU WILL NEED TO MAKE THE HEARTS AND ROSES IN ADVANCE.

Bows and Roses

You will need

- 10in (25cm) round, 4in (10cm) high cake covered in pale pink sugarpaste on a 14in (35cm) cake drum, covered in white sugarpaste. Set your cake at the back of the cake drum.
- 16in (40cm) double board covered in white sugarpaste
- 5in (12.5cm) round 3in (7.5cm) high cake on a 5in (12.5cm) thin card covered in white sugarpaste

- 2lb (900g) white sugarpaste mixed with 3oz (90g) pastillage (mix this together just before you want to use it)
- 2½oz (60g) pastillage
- Royal icing
- Pink paste or powder food colour
- 22-gauge white flower wires
- Textured rolling pin

Continued on page 69

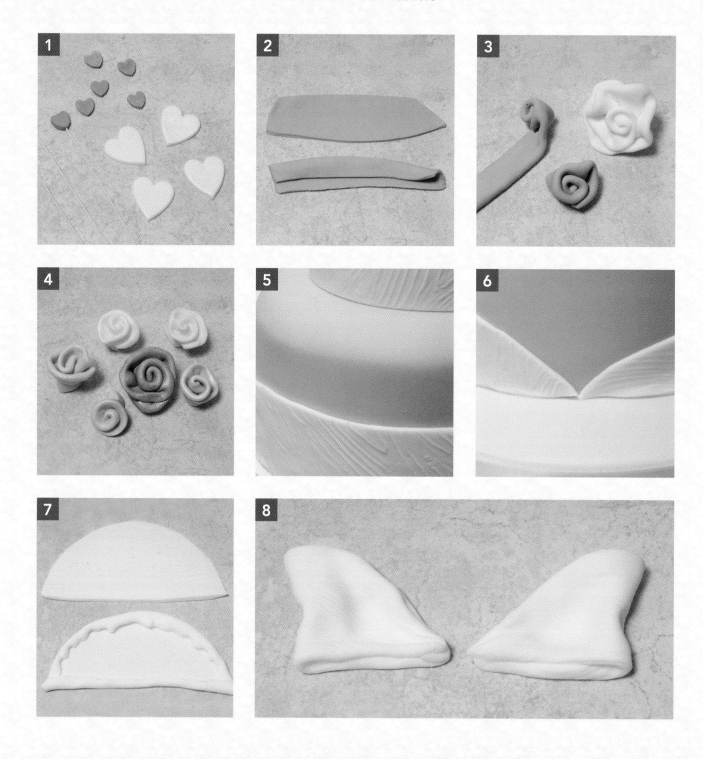

Continued from page 66

- Small and medium heart cutters
- Pearl lustre spray
- Paper piping bags
- Plastic dowelling

ADVANCE PREPARATION

Prepare steps one to four 48 hours before you require the cake to allow the hearts and roses to dry.

1 Mix 1oz (30g) of pastillage into a dark pink colour. Cut ten to twelve small heart shapes and insert a white wire into each heart; dip your wire into sugar glue before inserting it. Roll out 1oz (30g) of pastillage and cut three to five white medium hearts and place these on to wires too. Roll your paste in both pink and white colours a little thinner and cut out lots more small and medium hearts. Allow to dry on a surface dusted with icing sugar.

2 To form the rolled roses, use a little of the sugarpaste/pastillage mixture and colour it if required. Roll out a strip of the icing ⅛–⅙in (3–4mm) thick, 1½in (4cm) wide and 3–5in (7.5–12.5cm) long. Fold the strip over but do not squash it.

3 Start to roll the rose, pinching the base together as you go along to hold it together. Don't roll it too neatly or tightly; ripples and folds will improve the look of the flower. Repeat and form flowers of different sizes and colours.

4 Allow the roses to dry standing up on their chunky bases. When they have dried, spray them with pearl lustre spray to make them look shimmery.

BOW

5 Dowel the bottom tier of your cake (see 'Dowelling a cake', page 163). Place on the top tier towards the back and secure with a little royal icing. Roll out a length of white sugarpaste/pastillage mixture long enough to go around your top tier. Roll over the piece with a textured rolling pin and cut a strip 1in (2.5cm) wide. Stick it around your cake with sugar glue or apricot purée. Repeat around the bottom tier with a 1½in (4cm) wide strip.

6 Make sure the second strip begins and ends at the front of the cake. Cut each end piece so that it slopes downwards meeting the other end at a point ready for the bow to be added.

7 Roll out the paste mixture to a ⅛–⅙in (3–4mm) thickness, texture with the rolling pin and cut the half-circle shape shown on page 173. Flip the piece over and gently fold the edge in all the way around to form a hem.

8 Fold it from right to left so that the points meet; push in a dent at the folded end. Repeat the process to form the other one and fold this one from left to right.

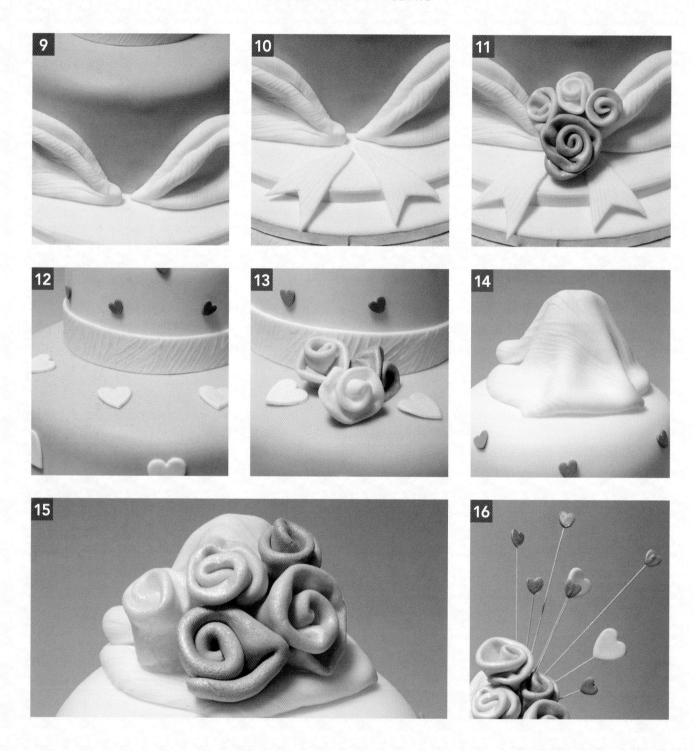

9 Stick each side of the bow to the cake with a generous quantity of royal icing to ensure that it stays in place. Mark a few little lines with the back of a knife at the middle of the bow.

10 Use the template on page 173 to cut the bow ends from your paste mixture. Remember to texture the surface of your icing with the rolling pin before you cut the shapes. Stick each one on the board with royal icing.

11 Pinch off the backs of your roses as you stick each one on your cake. Place the largest flower on first at the bottom, stick with royal icing and now stick the other three on top of it.

FINISHING OFF

12 Third-fill a piping bag with royal icing and carefully stick the small pink hearts on to the top tier and the larger white hearts on to the cake below.

13 Arrange a selection of roses on the top of the pink cake, resting against the white band on the second tier. Stick in place with royal icing.

14 Place a mound of icing on top of your top tier. Roll out a 5in (12.5cm) disc of icing and texture the surface with the rolling pin. Tuck all the edges under and place it over the mound, sticking with sugar glue or royal icing.

15 While the icing is still soft, add the roses for the top arrangement. Start with the larger roses at the base and add the others all around. Secure them with royal icing.

16 Cut off the ends of the wires to the appropriate length and arrange the hearts in place by pushing the wires into the mound of icing. Either position them all going upwards or some pointing off to the side as illustrated.

THIS DRAPED FABRIC EFFECT GIVES YOU A SIMPLE YET CLASSIC
WEDDING CAKE. YOU COULD TRY AND MATCH THE PIPING ON THE
CAKE TO THE DESIGN ON THE WEDDING DRESS IF YOU LIKE.

Draped Cascade

You will need

- 9in (23cm) white iced cake set to the back of a 12in (30cm) cake drum on a 14in (35cm) double board. Set your cake at the back of the first board with at least 3in (8cm) of space at the front.
- 12oz (340g) white sugarpaste
- 1oz (30g) pastillage

- Royal icing
- No. 1.5 piping tube
- Paper piping bags
- Crystal beading
- Spray of sugar flowers on a long stem

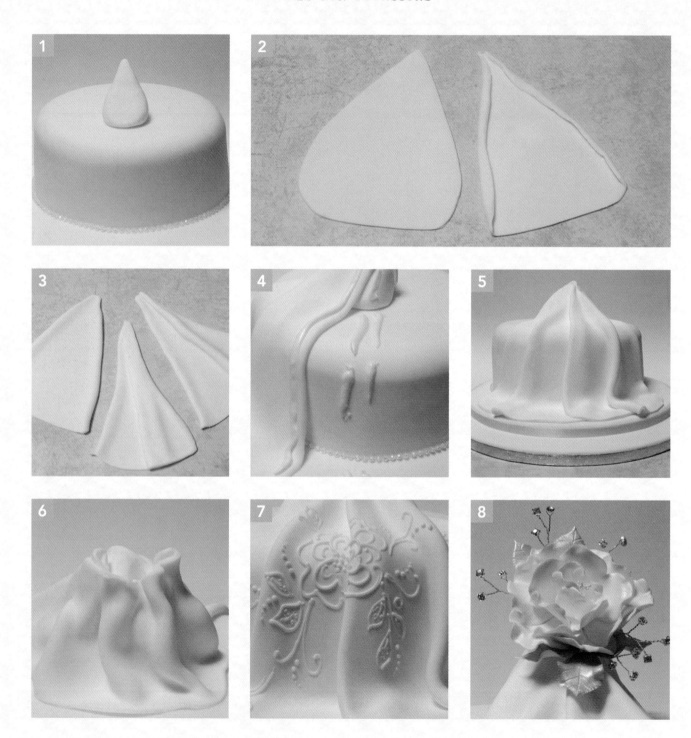

DRAPE

1 Arrange your crystal beading around the base of the cake and stick with royal icing. Place a 2in (5cm) cone of white sugarpaste on top of the cake slightly towards the front.

2 Mix the pastillage with all the remaining white sugarpaste. Roll out half of it into an 8in (20cm) long triangular shape ⅛in (3mm) thick. Cut the bottom corners off and fold all along each side to create a 'hem'.

3 Flip the piece of icing over and make one fold at the front of your drape from top to bottom. Fold from right to left.

4 Immediately stick the drape to the cake using a large quantity of piped royal icing to hold in place. Pipe a thick line of royal icing down the edge of the first piece and on the cone and cake ready to stick the second piece.

5 When the second piece of your drape is in place, press along the edges to secure and tweak all along the bottom edges of the frill so it doesn't lie flat.

6 Roll out a strip of the remaining icing 6in (15cm) long and 2in (5cm) wide. Tuck the ends under and make four folds along it. Stick it to the back of the cone with royal icing.

7 Allow the drape to dry for 24 hours before piping on it. Place a No. 1.5 piping tube into a small paper piping bag. Half-fill with royal icing and copy the piped pattern on page 74.

FINISHING OFF

8 Arrange your flower spray on top of your cake. The flowers will need a long spiky stem to push into the cone on the top of the cake.

TIP: *Fresh or silk flowers would be equally as effective on this cake.*

BIRTHDAY
CAKES

THIS DESIGN COULD ALSO BE ADAPTED INTO A LOVELY TWO-
OR THREE-TIER WEDDING CAKE. MAKE AS MANY BUTTERFLIES
AS YOU WISH AND PLACE THEM OVER THE CAKE AND BOARD.

Butterfly Ball

You will need

- 7in (18cm) round cake on a 10in (25cm) cake drum covered in white sugarpaste
- 12in (30cm) double board covered in lilac sugarpaste (polish all the surfaces with white satin shimmer)
- 3oz (90g) pastillage
- 2½oz (60g) white sugarpaste
- 2½oz (60g) lilac sugarpaste
- 8oz (225g) purple sugarpaste
- Pearl lustre spray

- Small and large butterfly cutters
- Patchwork cutters butterfly set
- Small piece of card
- 4in (10cm) round thin card
- ⅜in (8–10mm) silver dragees (balls)
- ¼in (6mm) silver dragees (balls)
- ⅛in (4mm) silver dragees (balls)

Continued on page 81

Continued from page 78

- Bulbous cone modelling tool
- 1¾in (6cm) round cutter
- Pink, turquoise and lilac colours
- Painting solution
- White satin shimmer
- Silvery moon shimmer

- Paper piping bags
- Paintbrushes
- Royal icing
- No. 1.5 piping tube
- Flat makeup sponge
- Disco white hologram edible glitter

ADVANCE PREPARATION

Prepare steps one to four 24 hours before you decorate the cake, to allow the butterflies to dry.

1 Roll out the pastillage on a work surface dusted with icing sugar to a thickness of ⅛–⅙in (3–4mm). Cut out large and small butterfly shapes. Immediately frill the outer edges of the wings (see 'How to frill sugarpaste', page 164).

TIP: *Remember to cut out some spare butterflies just in case you have any breakages.*

2 While the paste is still soft, press the patchwork butterfly cutter in to pattern the surface of the wings.

3 Now fold a piece of card at a 90-degree angle and rest your butterflies over it with the pattern facing downwards.

4 If you aren't confident about frilling your butterfly wings, just leave them plain; after you have cut them out, mark them with patchwork cutters.

BUTTERFLY DECORATION

5 When the butterflies are completely dry, paint the front. Mix your colour with white satin and painting solution to create a shimmering effect. You may need several coats.

6 When the front of the butterfly is dry, gently turn it over and paint the back too. Allow to dry.

7 Place a No. 1.5 piping tube into a small paper piping bag. Third-fill with royal icing and pipe a body and head on to the butterfly. The body is a succession of balls with a larger one piped for the head.

8 Paint the edges of all the butterflies silver. Use silvery moon mixed with a little white satin and painting solution. Immediately after painting the silver, sprinkle it with glitter.

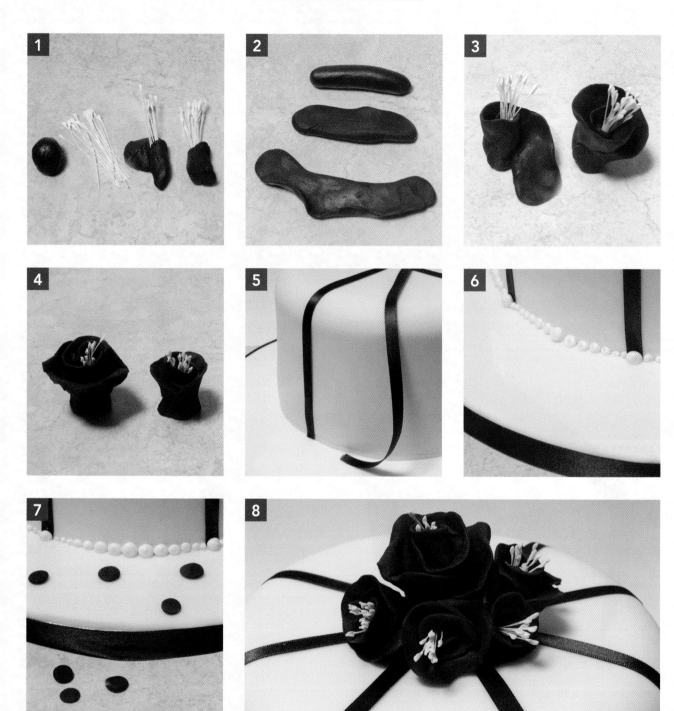

FLOWERS

1 Make a little bunch of cream stamens. Hold them in place with a ball of chocolate flavour sugarpaste formed into a squashed sausage and wrapped around them.

2 Form a 3in (7.5cm) sausage of chocolate flavour sugarpaste. Squash it flat then pinch it along one edge to thin and ripple it.

3 Twist it around the centrepiece with the thinned edge at the top. Wrap it loosely at the top and tightly at the base and pinch it around the bottom to hold.

4 Add additional strips of the chocolate flavour sugarpaste to create a larger flower. Allow your flowers to dry upright.

RIBBONS AND DOTS

5 Cut eight pieces of ribbon to go over your cake. Fix the first four with little dots of royal icing to secure. Add the final four strips. Stick a brown ribbon around the cake drum.

6 Place a No. 2 piping tube into a small paper piping bag. Third-fill with cream royal icing and pipe a large bead at the base of each ribbon. Pipe in between the ribbon around the base – start with the largest piped bead in the centre and decrease the sizes as you pipe away from it.

7 Make lots of little balls of chocolate flavour sugarpaste and squash them on to the board; if they don't stick by themselves, use a little brushed-on sugar glue.

FINISHING OFF

8 Pinch off the ends of your chocolate flowers and arrange them in a large bunch in the centre of your cake, sticking them down with dark brown royal icing.

TIP: *If you are short of time, use silk flowers on your cake instead of sugar ones.*

THIS CAKE DESIGN CAN BE USED AT CHRISTMAS AS WELL AS FOR
BIRTHDAYS. JUST CHANGE THE COLOURS TO SUIT THE THEME OF
THE OCCASION. ALLOW TIME FOR THE DECORATIONS TO DRY.

Perfect Parcels

You will need

- 12in (30cm) silver cake drum
- 2 x 4in (10cm) square cakes 3in (7.5cm) high covered in Atlantic blue sugarpaste
- 1 x 2in (5cm) cube white sugarpaste
- 1oz (30g) white Regal ice
- 3oz (90g) pastillage
- 2½oz (60g) white sugarpaste
- 1oz (30g) pale grey sugarpaste
- 4½oz (120g) Atlantic blue sugarpaste
- White and dark blue royal icing

- Silver dragees (balls)
- Painting solution
- White satin shimmer
- Silvery moon lustre powder
- Pearl lustre spray
- Selection of silver ribbons
- Paper piping bags
- Paintbrushes

Continued on page 91

88

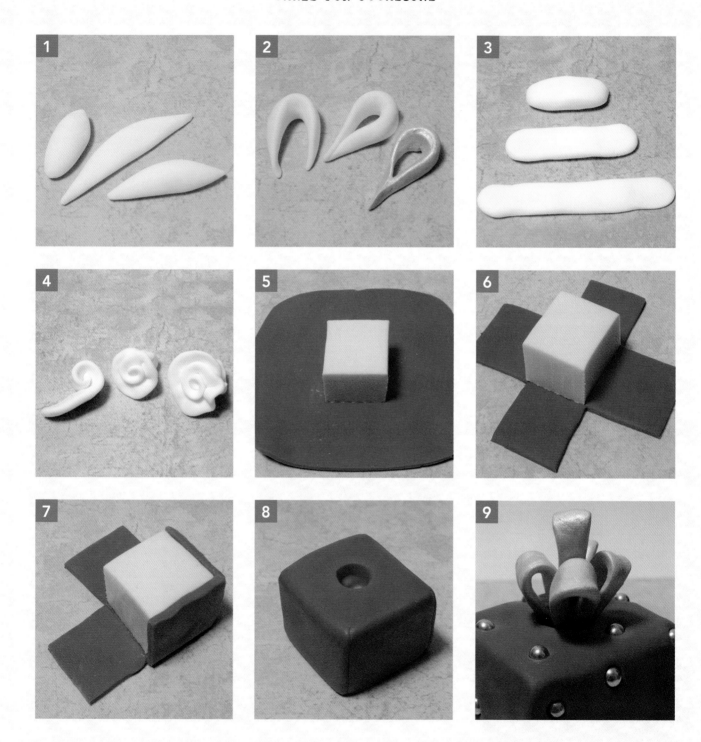

Continued from page 88
- Makeup sponge
- Small funky flower cutter
- No. 1 piping tube
- Bulbous cone modelling tool
- Guide to Sizes chart (see page 165)

ADVANCE PREPARATION

Prepare steps one to four 24 hours before you decorate the cakes to allow the roses to dry.

1 Form a small ball, size E, of white pastillage into a sausage shape, taper it at both ends and flatten very slightly with the palm of your hand.

2 Fold it over and tightly pinch the ends together; make seven to eight more. Allow to dry for at least 24 hours. Paint them all with silvery moon lustre powder mixed with a little painting solution.

3 Mix the 1oz (30g) of white Regal ice with ½oz (15g) of pastillage. Form a ball, size B, and shape it into a sausage 4–5in (10–12.5cm) long; squash it flat all along with the palm of your hand.

4 Start to roll it from one end, pinching the base together as you go along; don't roll too tightly and allow pleats and folds to form in your flower.

DOTTY PARCEL

5 Roll out the blue sugarpaste to a circle 7in (18cm) round. Firmly stick the white block of sugarpaste to the centre with brushed-on apricot purée.

TIP: *Ensure that your block of white sugarpaste has been set for at least 48 hours before you cover it with the coloured sugarpaste.*

6 Cut away the squares at each corner as illustrated, leaving the four pieces remaining to fold upwards.

7 Brush each of the four flaps with apricot purée and fold them upwards one at a time, sticking firmly; pinch the corners gently together.

8 Smooth over all the sides and corners with the palms of your hands to hide the joins. When the cube is finished neatly make a very large deep hole in the middle with the pointed end of the modelling tool.

9 While your blue icing is still soft, firmly push in lots of silver dragees deep enough for them to stay. Pipe a small amount of blue royal icing into the centre of the hole and push in as many silver loops as you can.

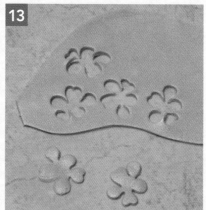

RIBBON PARCEL

10 Start to arrange your silver ribbons on one of the larger cakes. Stick with the barest minimum of royal icing, as too much will show through the fabric.

11 Parallel lines of different ribbons will look very effective and make a nice change from two pieces crossing over each other.

12 Form some of the remaining blue sugarpaste into five balls: one large, two medium and two small. Stick them all along the wide ribbon with a little blue royal icing to secure.

ROSES PARCEL

13 Mix the 1oz (30g) of the pale grey sugarpaste with a little ball of pastillage and roll out very thinly. Polish all over the surface with white satin shimmer on a makeup sponge. Cut out 12 small funky flower shapes.

14 Arrange two bands of silver ribbon across your cake and stick three flower shapes in each quarter using a little brushed-on apricot purée or sugar glue to secure them in place.

15 Place a No. 1 piping tube into a small piping bag. Fill with royal icing and pipe all around each flower with a thin line and add a group of dots in the centre.

16 Finally, add your large rolled rose to the top of your cake, using royal icing to stick in place.

FINISHING OFF
Either arrange your three presents on one board or display them individually.

WHAT MORE COULD YOU WANT FOR YOUR BIRTHDAY THAN THREE
FANTASTIC NEW HANDBAGS! REMEMBER TO ALLOW THE HANDLE
TIME TO DRY IN ADVANCE.

Handbag Heaven

You will need

- 7in (18cm) fruit cake cut in half, placed with the cut side at the base – marzipaned, and covered in pale grey sugarpaste on a 12in (30cm) round cake drum covered in white sugarpaste
- 4oz (115g) purple sugarpaste
- 12oz (340g) pink sugarpaste
- 1lb (450g) pale grey sugarpaste
- 2½oz (60g) pale grey pastillage
- Pale grey royal icing

- Pearl lustre spray
- Small silver dragees (balls)
- Paper piping bag
- Any small piping tube
- Design wheeler
- Quilting tool
- Bulbous cone modelling tool
- Guide to Sizes chart (see page 165)

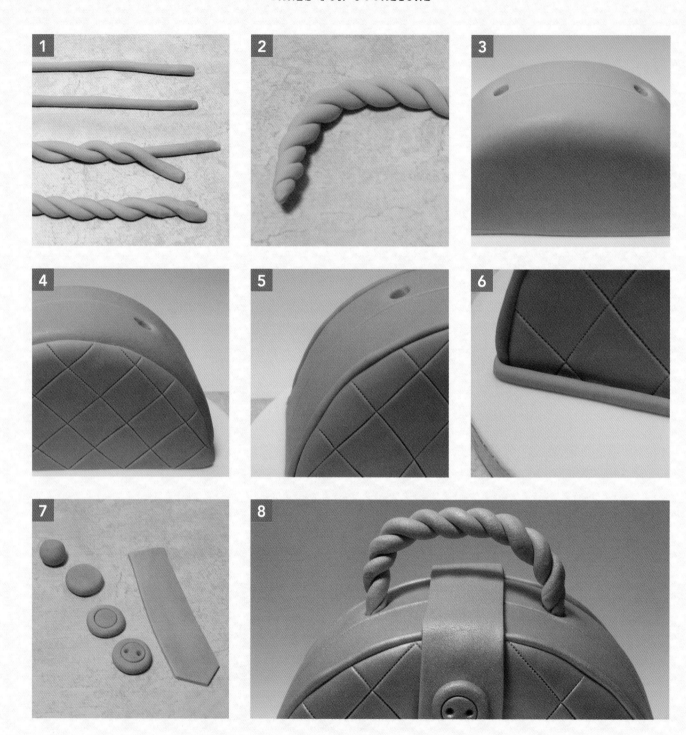

ADVANCE PREPARATION

Prepare steps one to two 48 hours before you require the cake to allow the handle to dry.

1 Divide the pale grey pastillage into two and roll out two sausages on a clean surface, 6–7in (15–18cm) in length. From the centre, wrap them around each other, working outwards.

TIP: *Do not use any icing sugar on your work surface when making a rope, as the dust will prevent the two pieces sticking together.*

2 Twist them together tightly to ensure they are stuck together, taper the ends into a point and bend the handle into a curve before it starts to set. Allow to dry for at least 48 hours.

GREY HANDBAG

3 Measure the distance between the two ends of the handle and make two large holes in the top of your handbag to correspond. With a knife, mark a line all along the top of the bag alongside the two holes.

4 Roll out an 8in (20cm) circle of pale grey sugarpaste on a work surface dusted with icing sugar. Cut it in half and stick one half on each side of the handbag; brushed-on apricot purée will hold it in place. Mark the lines on the surface with the quilting tool.

5 Roll out a very thin sausage of pale grey sugarpaste and stick it all along the edge of the quilted semi-circle. Repeat on the other side.

6 Roll out two 8in (20cm) long thin sausages of pale grey sugarpaste and stick one each side of the handbag along the base.

7 Form a button using a ball, size E, flatten slightly, then mark the circle with the large end of a piping tube and mark two holes in the middle. Cut the strap using the template on page 172.

8 Stick your strap over the top of the handbag and add your button to the front using sugar glue or apricot purée to secure. Pipe a little pale grey royal icing into the two holes and stick the handle in firmly. Spray your handbag all over with pearl lustre spray.

THIS IS THE PERFECT CAKE FOR A GARDENER. YOU COULD
EVEN ADD A FEW LETTUCES AND CARROTS (SEE 'HUNGRY BUNNIES',
PAGE 144). ALLOW TIME FOR THE FLOWERPOTS TO DRY.

Gardener's Delight

You will need

- 8 x 6in (20 x 15cm) oval cake 3in (7.5cm) high covered in green sugarpaste on a 11in (28cm) cake drum. Set the cake to the back.
- 4oz (115g) pastillage
- 2½oz (60g) black sugarpaste
- 4oz (115g) white sugarpaste
- 4oz (115g) pale grey sugarpaste
- 4oz (115g) mid-grey sugarpaste
- 4oz (115g) dark grey sugarpaste
- Piece of card

- Black and green royal icing
- Red food colour
- Chestnut food colour
- Silvery moon lustre powder
- Painting solution
- Soft brown sugar
- Raw spaghetti
- Paper piping bags

Continued on page 103

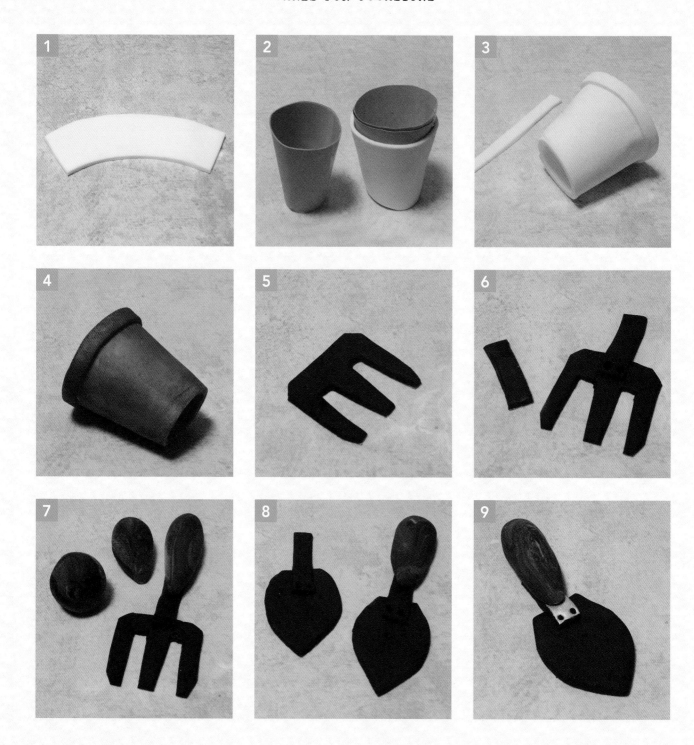

Continued from page 100
- No. 2 piping tube
- Paintbrushes
- Small stems of silk or sugar flowers
- Guide to Sizes chart (see page 165)

ADVANCE PREPARATION
Prepare steps one to four 48 hours before you require the cake to allow the flowerpot to dry.

1 Roll out the pastillage into a strip ⅛–⅛in (3–4mm) thick and cut the shape shown on page 172 for the flowerpot.

2 Wrap it around a piece of cardboard formed into the shape of a pot – make a second spare one too. Once it is dry, remove the cardboard from the centre.

3 Roll out a thin strip of pastillage. Cut a neat length ⅛in (4mm) thick and wrap it around the top of the pot, sticking with sugar glue.

4 Paint the pot all over with a mixture of red and brown colours mixed with painting solution. Allow to dry.

TOOLS
5 Mix the remaining pastillage with black sugarpaste. Roll out a piece ⅛in (2–3mm) thick and cut out the fork shape (see Templates, page 172).

6 Cut a little piece for the middle of the handle, and then stick it on to the fork with a little sugar glue. Press in two holes with a piece of raw spaghetti where the two pieces overlap.

7 Form the fork handle from a ball of dark grey sugarpaste, size D, and stick it in place.

8 Cut the trowel shape using the template on page 172. Follow steps six and seven to complete the tool.

9 Paint the middle section of both tools with silver paint – silvery moon lustre powder mixed with painting solution. Don't paint into the two holes.

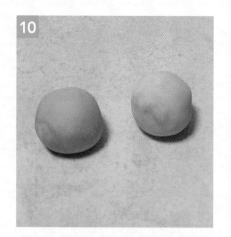

PATH

10 Mix up three colours of grey sugarpaste: one light, one dark and one medium in colour. Brush your board all over with sugar glue or apricot purée.

11 Start to squash balls of the different colours all over the board, use varying sizes and thicknesses and overlap them. Start to stick big stepping stones up the side of the cake.

12 Continue the path all the way up over the cake, then arrange your trowel on the path at the front.

FLOWERPOT

13 Push a ball of paste into the bottom of the flowerpot to plug it, then fill with soft brown sugar. When you put the pot on the cake, sprinkle some on the cake as well.

ANTS

14 Place a No. 2 piping tube into a small paper piping bag. Fill with black royal icing. Paint six little black legs on the side of the cake and pipe three balls for the body of the ant.

GRASS

15 Using green royal icing in a small piping bag, pipe grass (see 'Piping grass', page 168).

FINISHING OFF

16 To make your cake look more feminine, a nice touch would be to add some small stems of silk or sugar flowers.

THIS WOULD BE GREAT FOR A CHILD OR ADULT. JUST CHANGE THE COLOURS TO THE TEAM THEY SUPPORT. YOU COULD ALSO PUT THE AGE OF THE CHILD OR ADULT ON THE BACK OF THE SHIRT.

Soccer Crazy

You will need

- 6in (15cm) round cake 4in (10cm) high sponge shaved into a ball shape and covered with white sugarpaste on a 12in (30cm) cake drum
- 4oz (115g) black sugarpaste
- 2½oz (60g) white sugarpaste
- 2½oz (60g) peach sugarpaste
- 10oz (280g) green sugarpaste
- 6½oz (180g) red sugarpaste

- Black, green and brown royal icing
- Raw spaghetti
- Bulbous cone modelling tool
- Paper piping bags
- No. 1 piping tube
- Cocktail stick or toothpick
- Guide to Sizes chart (see page 165)

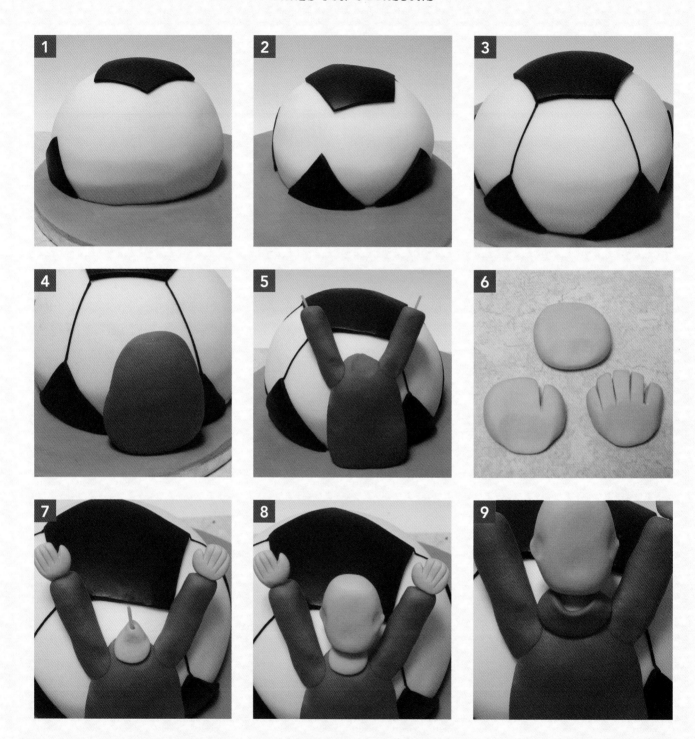

SOCCER BALL

1 Place your white-covered cake to the back of the cake drum. Cover the cake drum in green sugarpaste. Cut a big black hexagon (see Templates, page 172) and stick it to the top of the ball. Cut and add a black triangle to the base of the ball (see Templates, page 172).

2 Cut four more black triangles and stick them around the base of the cake with sugar glue or apricot purée.

3 Place a No. 1 piping tube into a small paper piping bag. Fill with a little black royal icing and pipe lines connecting the black shapes.

SOCCER PLAYER

4 Form a body, size A, from red sugarpaste and shape it into a narrow cone, then squash it and stick to the front of the ball.

5 Form two arms, each size C and 2½in (7cm) in length. Stick one each side of the body pointing upwards from the shoulders. Push a piece of raw spaghetti into each arm, leaving ¼in (5mm) showing at the top.

6 Form the two hands from a squashed ball of peach sugarpaste. Mark the thumb with a deep cut, then add three lines to the side.

7 Pop each hand on top of the spaghetti at the end of each arm; push them on firmly so there is no gap showing. The neck is a ball of peach sugarpaste, size F. Form it into a cone shape and stick it at the top of the body between the arms. Push a piece of raw spaghetti into the neck and down through the body.

8 Shape a flesh-coloured ball, size C, into a smooth oval shape. Impress the ear shapes with the end of the modelling tool and place the head on to the spaghetti.

9 Add a little red collar from a 1½in (6cm) sausage of red sugarpaste, squashed flat then wrapped around the neck.

Guide to sizes	
Body	A
Arms	2 x C
Hands	2 x F
Neck	F
Collar	F
Head	C

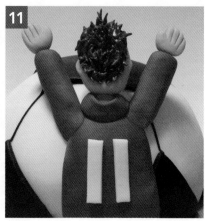

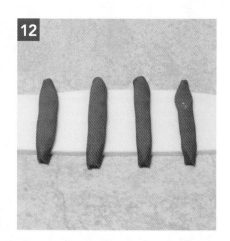

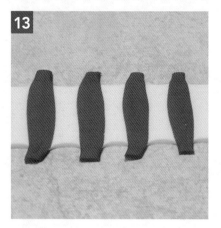

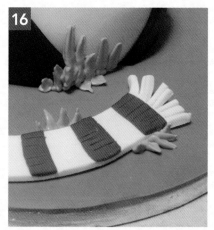

10 Half-fill a small piping bag with dark brown royal icing, cut the end of the bag as illustrated on page 168 and give your footballer a long spiky hair style, as shown on page 169.

11 Roll out a small piece of white sugarpaste on a work surface dusted with icing sugar. Cut two little strips and stick them to the back of the football shirt to make a number 11.

SCARF

12 Roll out a sausage of white sugarpaste 6in (15cm) long and 1½in (4cm) wide. Squash six or seven little sausages of red icing across it at equal intervals.

13 Roll over the strip to press the red pieces into the white sugarpaste; this will flatten and stick them at the same time.

14 Put a straight line down each side – make five or six cuts at each end of the scarf and scratch some little lines all down its length with a cocktail stick.

15 Arrange the scarf at the front of the cake along the green base, sticking with a little sugar glue.

16 Using green royal icing in a small piping bag, pipe grass up the sides of the ball (see 'Piping grass', page 168) and a few patches on the base.

CHILDREN'S CAKES

WHAT A LOVELY SURPRISE, A JACK-IN-A-BOX JUMPING
OUT OF YOUR CAKE! BE SURE TO ALLOW TIME FOR THE BOX
TO DRY BEFORE YOU FINISH YOUR CAKE.

Jack-in-a-Box

You will need

- 7in (17.5cm) square cake covered in red sugarpaste on an 11in (27.5cm) square cake drum covered in yellow sugarpaste
- 3½in (9cm) square sponge cake 3in (7.5cm) high on a 3½in (9cm) thin card
- 1lb (450g) blue sugarpaste
- 1lb (450g) green sugarpaste
- 4oz (115g) white sugarpaste
- 4oz (115g) white sugarpaste
- 3oz (90g) yellow sugarpaste

- 1oz (30g) red sugarpaste
- 1oz (30g) orange sugarpaste
- Filling cream
- 8oz (225g) royal icing
- 6½oz (180g) pastillage
- ½ teaspoon tylo powder
- Orange paste colour
- Dark blue paste colour

Continued on page 117

POP ANY LITTLE ANIMALS INTO THIS BED IF YOU LIKE. YOU CAN ADD MORE BEARS OR OTHER ANIMALS, BUT JUST MAKE SURE THAT YOU ADD EXTRA BODIES AND DENTS IN THE PILLOW.

Bedtime Bears

You will need

- 7in (18cm) square cake covered in pale yellow sugarpaste on a 10in (25cm) square drum covered in yellow sugarpaste
- 1lb (450g) white sugarpaste
- 8oz (225g) lilac sugarpaste
- 1oz (30g) yellow sugarpaste
- 4oz (115g) teddy-bear brown sugarpaste
- 12oz (340g) dark brown sugarpaste

- Liquorice black paste colour
- Bulbous cone modelling tool
- Quilting tool
- Large star cutter
- Small star cutter
- Paintbrushes
- Cocktail stick or toothpick
- Guide to Sizes chart (see page 165)

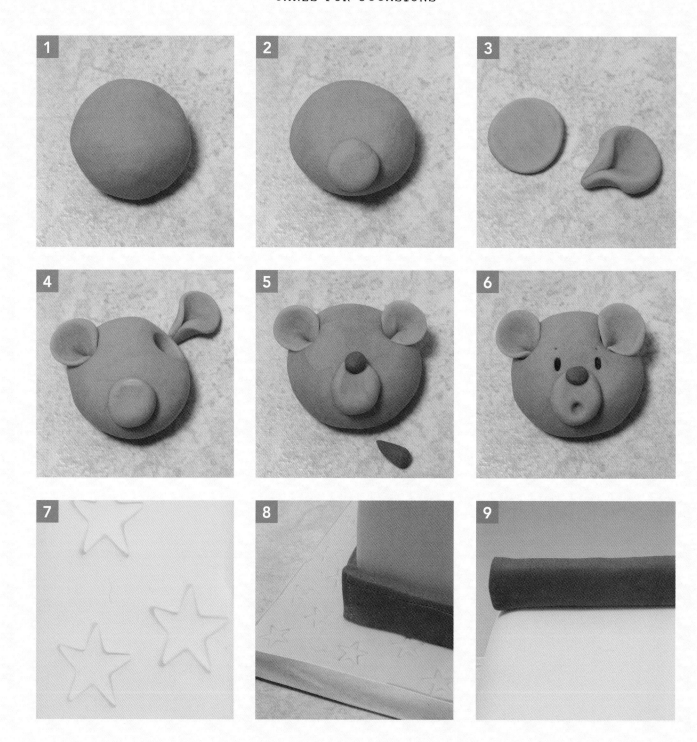

BEAR

1 Form a smooth ball, size C, in teddy-bear brown sugarpaste and place it on your work surface to flatten the back.

2 Press a small ball, size G, down firmly on to the lower part of the head; it should stick by itself.

3 Shape a ball, size G, into an ear. Flatten it first and pinch one side together. Repeat for the second ear.

4 Make two extremely large holes at the top of the head and place an ear in each one. Gently push the pointed end of the tool into the centre of each ear to secure.

5 Make a hole at the top of the flattened nose (snout). Form a teardrop-shaped nose from a ball, size H, in dark brown sugarpaste and firmly push the point into the hole and flatten slightly.

6 Make a little hole for the mouth and mark the eyes with black paste colour (see 'Eyes', page 166). With the gentlest touch, add two tiny dots for the eyebrows.

BED

7 When you cover the cake drum in yellow sugarpaste, press little star shapes all over the icing with a large star cutter.

8 Roll out and cut a thick strip of dark brown sugarpaste 1in (2.5cm) wide. Stick it all round the base of the cake with sugar glue, then run along the top and edges with a quilting tool.

9 Using all the remaining dark brown sugarpaste, roll a sausage 7½in (19cm) long and flatten it slightly. Cut each end straight and stick it at the top of the bed for the headboard.

Guide to sizes	
Head	*C*
Nose	*G*
Nose tip	*H*
Ears	*2 x G*

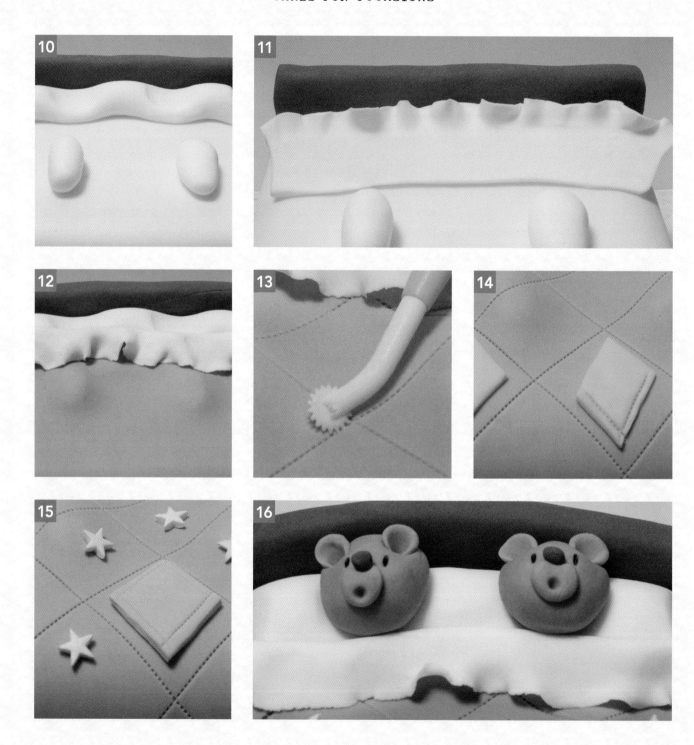

10 Form a white sausage shape 7in (18cm) long. Cut the ends straight, place the pillow in the bed and press in two dents ready for the heads. Add two sausage-shaped bodies.

11 Now roll out a strip of white sugarpaste ⅛in (2–3mm) thick, 8in (20cm) long and 1in (2.5cm) wide. Frill all the way along one side (see page 164) and place it in the bed, covering the pillow. Stick down the straight side with apricot purée.

12 Brush the top of your cake with apricot purée. Roll out an 8in (20cm) square of lilac sugarpaste ⅛in (3mm) thick. Place on the bed and fold the white frill down over the top edge. Pinch all the way around the edge to thin it.

13 Using the quilting tool, make a diamond-shaped pattern all over the top of the bedspread by gently rolling the wheel.

14 Roll out and cut several yellow diamond shapes to stick on top of your quilt. Run around the edge of your diamonds with the quilting tool.

15 Cut out lots of little white stars and stick them all over the empty patches on your quilt. Stick with a dot of brushed-on sugar glue.

FINISHING OFF

16 Place your two little bear heads on to the pillow, sticking with a little sugar glue. More bear heads can be added but remember to add more bodies in the bed and dents in the pillow.

THIS CAKE IS PERFECT FOR PRINCESSES OF ALL AGES. IF YOU LIKE, FINISH IT WITH A LITTLE PINK SUGAR FAIRY (SEE FAIRY WISHES, PAGE 132). ALLOW PLENTY OF TIME TO MAKE THE CAKE.

Princess Castle

You will need

- 7in (18cm) round cake 3in (7.5cm) high covered with pink sugarpaste on a 12in (30cm) round cake drum
- 4in (10cm) round cake 1½in (4cm) high covered in pink sugarpaste
- 6½oz (180g) white sugarpaste
- 3oz (90g) pink pastillage
- 1oz (30g) white pastillage
- 1lb (455g) pale grey marbled sugarpaste

- Pale pink royal icing
- Lilac colour
- Pink colour
- Painting solution
- White satin lustre
- White satin shimmer
- Pearl lustre spray
- Disco white hologram edible glitter

Continued on page 129

THIS IS THE PERFECT BIRTHDAY CAKE FOR A YOUNG CHILD BURSTING WITH WISHES. MAKE SURE YOU ALLOW PLENTY OF TIME FOR THE WINGS AND WAND TO DRY.

Fairy Wishes

You will need

- 6in (15cm) cake on an 11in (28cm) round drum. The cake needs to be 3in (7.5cm) high and covered in pale pink sugarpaste
- 13in (33cm) cake drum covered in dark pink sugarpaste
- 2½oz (60g) white pastillage
- 8oz (225g) royal icing
- Yellow food colour
- Raw spaghetti
- 4oz (115g) skin-coloured sugarpaste
- 8oz (225g) dark pink sugarpaste
- 8oz (225g) light pink sugarpaste
- 8oz (225g) white sugarpaste
- Liquorice black paste colour
- Disco white hologram edible glitter
- White satin shimmer
- Paper piping bags
- No. 1.5 piping tube

Continued on page 135

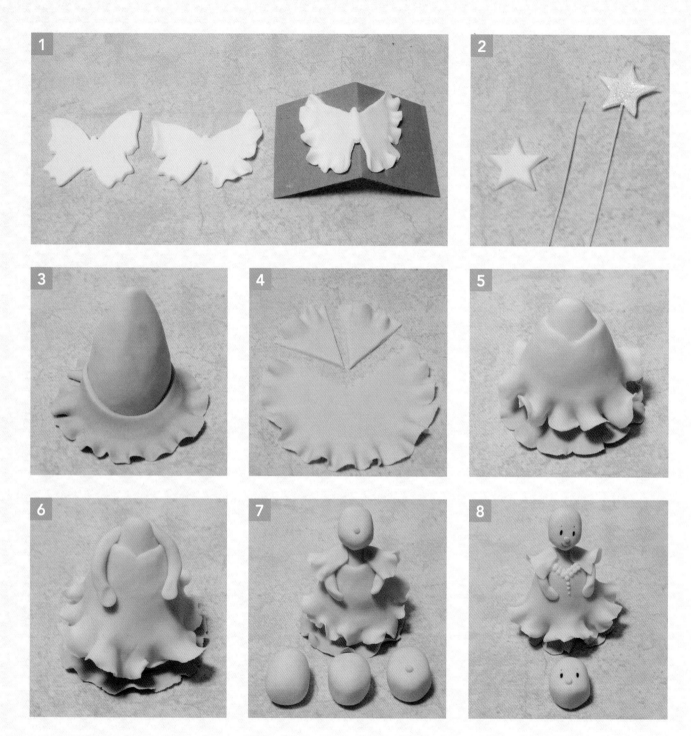

Continued from page 132
- Garrett frill cutter with removable centre
- Medium star cutter
- Large butterfly cutter
- 22-gauge white flower wires
- Polystyrene block
- Guide to Sizes chart (see page 165)

ADVANCE PREPARATION
Prepare steps one and two, wings and wand; allow them to dry for 24 hours before finishing your fairy – always make a few spares too.

1 Roll out the white pastillage to a thickness of ⅛in (2–3mm). Cut out one butterfly and immediately frill all along the outer edge of the wings (see 'How to frill sugarpaste', page 164). Bend your butterfly over a folded piece of card to dry overnight.

2 Cut some medium stars from your remaining pastillage and push a length of wire, dipped into sugar glue, into each star. Allow the stars to dry sticking in a polystyrene block.

Guide to sizes	
Body	**A**
Arms	**2 x F**
Head	**Small D**
Nose	**I**

FAIRY
3 Make a body for your fairy from a ball, size A, in skin-coloured sugarpaste. Form it into a cone shape 2in (5cm) high. Cut one garrett frill shape in dark pink and frill all around the edge (see 'How to frill sugarpaste', page 164). Cut the centre out and cut once to open it out. Wrap it around the base of the cone, sticking with royal icing or sugar glue.

4 Roll out the pale pink sugarpaste and cut out another frill. Frill it all around the edge, cut a third away and then cut that in half. The two little pieces will become the sleeves of the fairy, but cut the point off each one first.

5 Brush some sugar glue all around the top of the first frill. Wrap the second frill around the body with the join at the back.

6 Form a ball of skin-coloured sugarpaste, size F, into a thin sausage shape 1in (2.5cm) long. Flatten the end for the palm and pinch in a little wrist. Stick the arm to the shoulder just above the pink dress. Repeat for the second arm.

7 Stick the little frilled sleeves to the top of the arms. Form the head from an oval of skin-coloured sugarpaste, size small D. Gently pinch the chin into a soft point and insert a tiny nose, size I, into a hole in the face (see 'Heads', page 165). Push a piece of raw spaghetti into the body and stick the head down on to the spaghetti.

8 Mark the eyes with black paste colour (see 'Eyes', page 166). With the gentlest touch, add two tiny dots for the eyebrows. Mark the mouth (see page 166). When the head is in place, place a No. 1.5 piping tube into a small paper piping bag. Half-fill with royal icing and pipe the little decorative pearls at the neck of the fairy's dress.

9 Mix up some yellow hair-coloured royal icing, half-fill a small piping bag and pipe your fairy's hair following instructions on page 169. Make sure the royal icing is peaky and not wet and shiny because you want individual strands of hair to show.

10 Remove your wings from the cardboard when they are set and sponge white satin shimmer all over them to give them a glossy sheen. Pipe a line of royal icing at the back of the dress and firmly push the wings into the back of the fairy until they are stuck. Pipe a little line of pearls up the middle of the wings.

11 Brush one star wand with sugar glue and dip into the glitter. You want the fairy to hold her wand firmly – push the end of the wire right into her body just behind her hand so it looks like she is holding it.

FRILLS

12 Cut several frills from the darker pink colour. Frill following the instructions on page 164. If the frill keeps on sticking to your tool, leave the frill to dry out for a few minutes and try again. Cut the centre out and then slice it in half.

13 Mark seven dots around the bottom of your cake to indicate where the frills should begin and end. Pipe a thick band of royal icing in a loop and firmly press your first frill in place; tuck the ends down. The frill wants to be low enough to cover the join of the cake and board.

14 Continue all the way around your cake until you meet up with your first frill. Now prepare the paler pink frills. Pipe a thick band of icing at the very top of the dark pink frill and stick on the next row. Tuck all the ends down.

15 You are now ready to stick on the final layer of white frills. Follow all the stages as before but as this is the last layer, flick the ends of the frills outwards and away from each other, pinching them together tightly at the top.

FINISHING OFF

16 Using your piping bag with royal icing and the No. 1.5 tube, pipe a neat line of pearls all along the top edge of the white frill. Pipe a larger ball at the top of each point and finish with three smaller graduated dots going upwards. Mount your cake on the larger board and finish the edges with ribbon.

USING ALPHABET CUTTERS IS A GREAT WAY TO WRITE ON YOUR CAKE WITHOUT HAVING TO PIPE IN ROYAL ICING. IF YOU CAN'T FIND FLOWER PASTE FOR THE LETTERS, USE PASTILLAGE INSTEAD.

Alphabet Bear

You will need

- 8in (20cm) hexagonal cake covered in white icing on a 12in (30cm) cake drum covered in pale blue sugarpaste
- 6½oz (180g) pastillage
- 5½oz (150g) white sugarpaste
- 6½oz (180g) teddy-bear brown sugarpaste
- 1oz (30g) yellow sugarpaste and tiny ball of red sugarpaste for ducks (optional)
- 1oz (30g) flower paste or pastillage for the lettering
- Alphabet tappit set

- Black paste colour
- Selection of colours
- Small ball of chocolate-brown sugarpaste
- Royal icing
- Raw spaghetti
- Paper piping bags
- Bulbous cone modelling tool
- No. 1.5 piping tube

Continued on page 141

C
-
-
-

A
Pr
th

1
eig
fra
bu
br
wi

2
sti

C
E
B
L
A
F
E
N
D
E
F
E

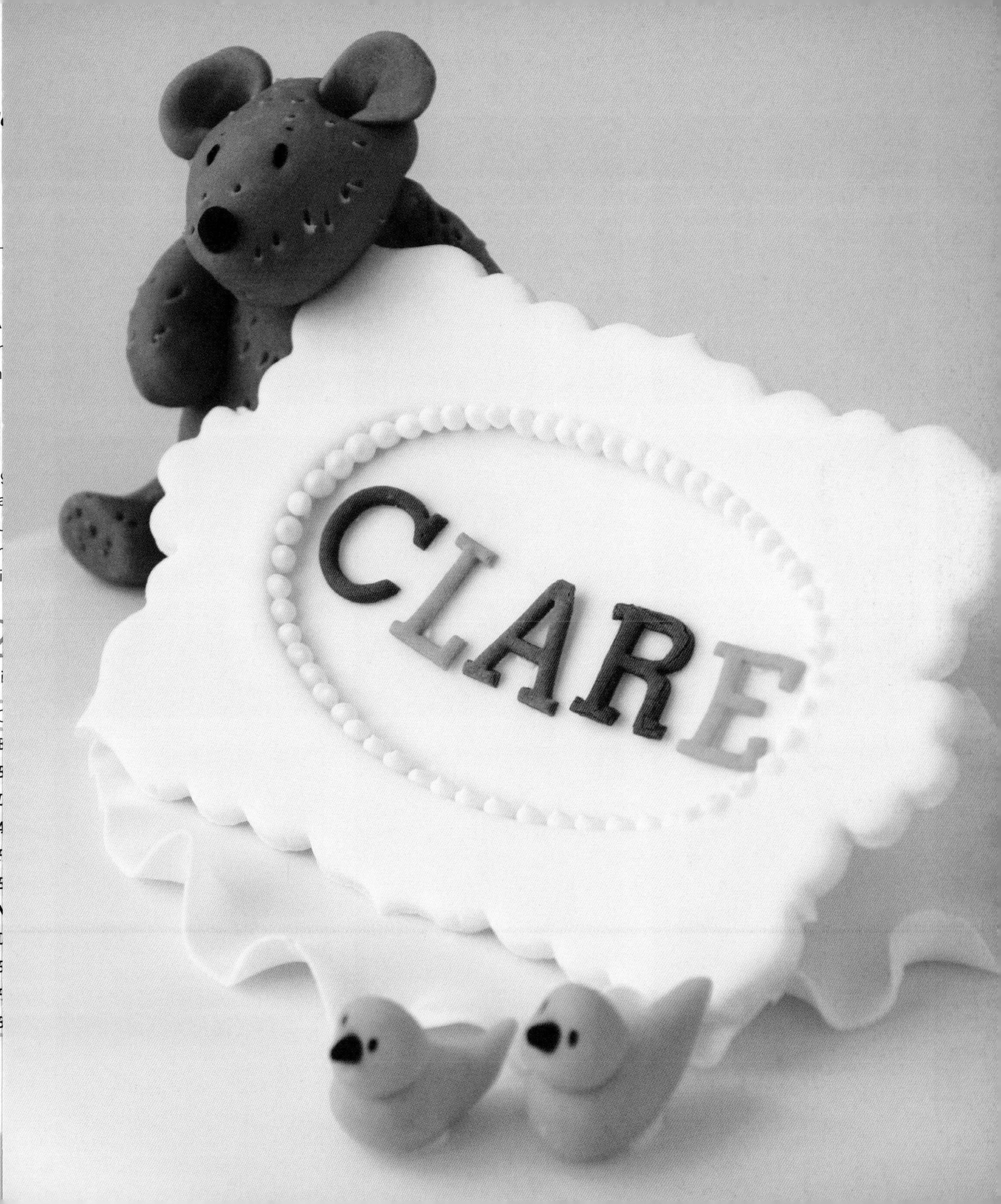

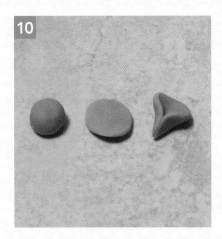

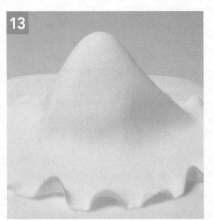

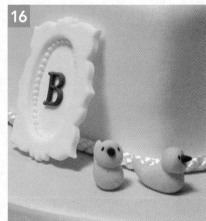

10 Shape each ear from a ball, size G, by squashing it and pinching on one side; repeat with the other ear.

11 Now pop the ears into the holes. If they don't stick by themselves, make the holes larger, and press the pointed end of the tool into the centre of each ear to secure. Insert a tiny teardrop shape of chocolate-brown sugarpaste into the hole for the nose, size I. Mark a belly button.

12 Mark the bear's eyes with black paste colour (See 'Eyes', page 166). Gently scratch your teddy all over with a cocktail stick to make him look fluffy and furry.

FINISHING OFF

13 Form a white cone shape made from a ball, size A. Place towards the back of your cake. Roll out a 5in (12.5cm) disc of white sugarpaste and frill around the edge (See 'How to frill sugarpaste', page 164). Stick this over the cone on top of the cake.

14 Using royal icing, stick a piece of twisted white braid around the base of your cake – use sticky tape over the cut ends to stop it unravelling. Rest the small frames against the cake sides, sticking with royal icing at the top.

15 Arrange your large frame and bear on the cake, rest it back against the blanket and position your teddy so that it looks like he is supporting the frame.

16 As an optional extra, you may want to add a few tiny ducks at the front of the cake (the instructions for making these are on page 51).

NOT ONLY IS THIS THE PERFECT CAKE FOR A CHILD, IT WOULD ALSO BE IDEAL FOR AN ADULT GARDENER. YOU DON'T NEED TO LIMIT IT TO VEGETABLES; YOU CAN MAKE FLOWERS TOO.

Hungry Bunnies

You will need

- 8 x 6in (20 x 15cm) oval cake on an 11in (28cm) round cake drum all covered in pale green sugarpaste and polished with white satin shimmer
- 8oz (225g) chocolate-brown sugarpaste
- 4oz (115g) bright green sugarpaste
- 2½oz (60g) orange sugarpaste
- 4oz (115g) very light brown sugarpaste
- 1oz (30g) white sugarpaste
- ¼ teaspoon tylo powder
- Liquorice black paste colour

- Chocolate sticks
- A little brown and pale green royal icing
- Paintbrush
- Cocktail sticks or toothpicks
- Straight frill cutter
- Bulbous cone modelling tool
- Small knife
- Paper piping bags
- Green ribbon
- Guide to Sizes chart (see page 165)

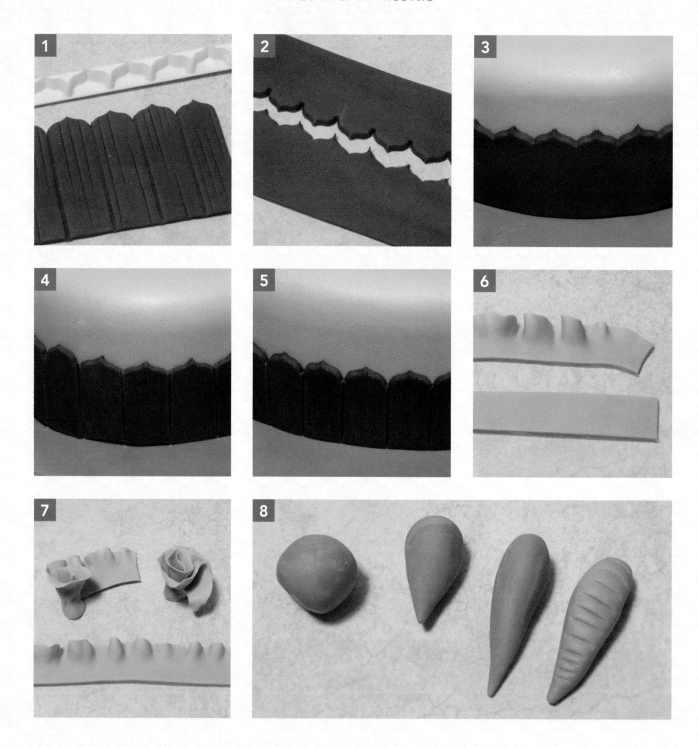

FENCE

1 Mix together the tylo powder with a quarter of the chocolate-brown sugarpaste and roll it out to a ⅙in (4mm) thickness. Cut a 4in (10cm) strip 3in (7.5cm) in width, then cut along the top edge with the straight frill cutter. You want five pointed sections along the top. Mark the lines on it with the back of a knife. Allow to dry on a work surface dusted with icing sugar.

2 Roll out a 5in (12.5cm) wide strip with the remaining chocolate-brown sugarpaste. Use the straight frill cutter to cut neatly through the middle of the entire length.

3 Use a large brush to paint apricot purée all over the lower part of your cake's side. Stick the fence all the way around the sides, joining the two ends neatly at the back of the cake.

4 Use the back of a knife or a straight edge to mark deep lines in between each section of the fence panels; do not press too hard as you don't want to cut through completely.

5 With the tip of a sharp knife or cocktail stick, make little scratches all up the sides in between the deep lines.

VEGETABLES

6 Roll out a long piece of bright green sugarpaste on a work surface dusted with icing sugar. Cut a 1in (2.5cm) wide strip and start to frill all along one side with the modelling tool (see 'How to frill sugarpaste', page 164).

7 When you have frilled along the whole length, carefully roll up short sections for small lettuces and long sections for larger lettuces. Pinch them tightly at the base when you have finished rolling and allow to dry standing upright.

8 Form a little orange carrot from a small ball of sugarpaste. Shape it into a long cone and mark little horizontal lines with a knife all the way down its length. Make 10 to 15 carrots.

Guide to sizes	
LARGE BUNNY	
Body	*B*
Front legs	*E*
Head	*D*
Tail	*F*
Nose	*I*
SMALL BUNNY	
Body	*D*
Front legs	*F*
Head	*E*
Tail	*G*
Nose	*J*
Nose	*H*

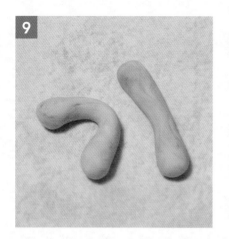

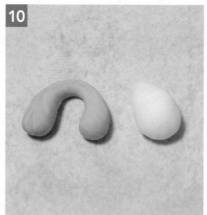

BUNNIES

9 Using light brown sugarpaste, form the front legs of the large bunny from a ball, size E. Shape into a sausage 1in (2.5cm) long and roll slightly to thin in the middle; fold around in a 'U' shape.

10 Form a size F ball of white sugarpaste into a cone shape, then flatten the pointed end ready for the body to sit neatly on top of it. Also flatten the curve on the piece for the legs.

11 Form your body, size B, into a fat cone shape. Firmly stick this on to the tail and legs with them poking out at both ends. Use sugar glue to secure if necessary.

12 To make the head, shape a ball, size D, into a long pointed cone, cut a long line to separate the ears and mark a faint line up each one. Bend outwards at the top. Mark the whisker lines before adding the nose, which is a brown teardrop shape, size I, pushed into a hole. Mark the eyes (see 'Eyes', page 166) with black paste colour after the head is on the body.

13 When you have made the head, use sugar glue to stick it on the body sloping backwards. Now make two small bunnies and lots of little extra bunny heads on their own.

FINISHING OFF

14 Stick three chocolate sticks into the top of your cake in a straight row towards the back; push them in so that they are slightly lower than the fence panel height. Rest your spare fence panel against the sticks and hold in place with a little piped brown royal icing at the back.

15 Start to place your lettuces and carrots on the cake; you could also add other vegetables and even flowers. Arrange some on the board too, sticking with royal icing. Add a few extra chocolate sticks where necessary.

16 Pipe a little royal icing at the top of the fence in several places and stick on your bunny heads, peeping over. Stick on your large and small bunnies. Finish with a ribbon around the cake drum.

To create the decorated cakes in this book you will require the equipment and ingredients listed on the following spread. You will see that product codes are provided after many of the items. Please refer to the list of suppliers on pages 174–175 for details.

First, however, you must prepare your cake; therefore a range of recipes are provided on the following pages. In addition, you will find all the information and advice you'll need to be able to make a variety of cake models. If you decide to have a go at making models, make sure you practise the simpler ones first before you attempt the more complicated characters, and always use the Guide to Sizes chart provided on page 165 to ensure they are in proportion.

There is such a wide range of cakes within this book that I'm sure you'll be able to find a design to suit your occasion. Don't be afraid to adapt a design or develop the ideas with your own finishing touches!

CAKE
BASICS

Equipment

1 Quilting tool (PME)

2 Bulbous cone modelling tool (PME)

3 Design wheeler (PME)

4 Oval cutters (PME)

5 Rolling pin

6 Crimper (closed curve) (PME)

7 Piping tube (PME)

8 Garrett frill cutter (PME)

9 Plastic dowelling

10 Frame cutters – various (AP/GP)

11 Small daisy/marguerite cutter (PME)

12 Funky flower cutters (AP/GP)

13 Holly leaf cutter (PME)

14 Alphabet tappit set (FMM)

15 Butterfly patchwork cutters (PC)

16 Large snowflake cutters (TALA)

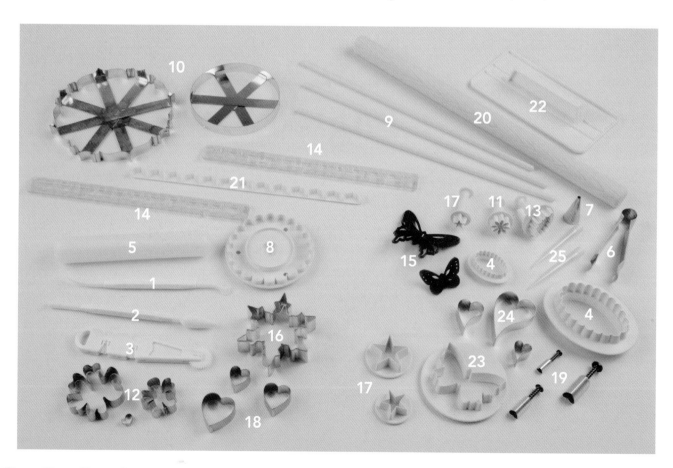

Ingredients

17 Star cutters/plungers (PME)

18 Heart cutters (PME)

19 Heart plungers (PME)

20 Textured rolling pin (HP)

21 Straight frill cutter (FMM)

22 Smoother (FMM)

23 Butterfly cutter (PME)

24 Funky heart cutters (FC)

25 Posy picks

You will also need:

Piping bags

Cocktail sticks or toothpicks

Paintbrushes

Small knife and scissors

22-gauge white flower wires

Cream stamens

Large plaque cutters (AP/GP)

Various ribbons

Doily cutter (JEM)

Small plaque cutter (PME/AP/GP)

Small blossom cutter (PME)

Small, flat make-up sponge

Round-headed pins

- White sugarpaste/rolled fondant
- Coloured sugarpaste/chocolate sugarpaste
- Marzipan
- Liquorice black paste colour
- Paste food colours – various
- Icing sugar
- Royal icing
- Filling cream
- Tylo powder
- Chocolate sticks
- Piping gel
- Pastillage
- Sugar glue
- Apricot purée
- Silver/gold dragees (balls) (LC)
- Lustre powders (EA)
- Raw spaghetti
- Soft brown sugar
- Sprays of sugar flowers
- Disco white hologram edible glitter (EA)
- Pearl Lustre spray (PME)

Note: Letters in brackets refer to suppliers. See Suppliers on pages 174–175.

Fruit cake quantities Oven temperature: 275°F/140°C/Gas mark 1.5 for ALL sizes

Tin Size	Round 4in (10cm)	Round 5in (12.5cm) Square 4in (10cm)	Round 6in (15cm) Square 5in (12.5cm)	Round 7in (18cm) Square 6in (15cm)
Dried fruit	9oz (255g)	12oz (340g)	15oz (425g)	1lb 2oz (510g)
Glacé cherries	1½oz (45g)	2½oz (60g)	2¾oz (75g)	3oz (90g)
Rum or sherry	4 tablespoons	5 tablespoons	6 tablespoons	7 tablespoons
Lemon rind and juice	¼	½	½	1
Unsalted butter	2½oz (60g)	3oz (90g)	3½oz (100g)	4oz (115g)
Dark soft brown sugar	1½oz (45g)	2½oz (60g)	2¾oz (75g)	3oz (90g)
Baking powder	¼ teaspoon	¼ teaspoon	¼ teaspoon	¼ teaspoon
Plain flour	3½oz (100g)	4oz (115g)	4½oz (130g)	5oz (140g)
Grated nutmeg	¼ teaspoon	¼ teaspoon	¼ teaspoon	¼ teaspoon
Mixed spice	¼ teaspoon	¼ teaspoon	¼ teaspoon	¼ teaspoon
Cinnamon	¼ teaspoon	½ teaspoon	½ teaspoon	½ teaspoon
Medium eggs	2	2	2½	3
Black treacle	1 teaspoon	2 teaspoons	2 teaspoons	2 teaspoons
Cooking time (hours)	1¼–1½	1¾–2½	2½–3	About 3

Madeira cake quantities Oven temperature: 325°F/160°C/Gas mark 3 for ALL sizes

Tin Size	Round 5in (12.5cm) Square 4in (10cm)	Round 6in (15cm) Square 5in (12.5cm)	Round 7in (18cm) Square 6in (15cm)
Softened butter	2½oz (60g)	3oz (90g)	4½oz (130g)
Margarine	2½oz (60g)	3oz (90g)	4½oz (130g)
Caster sugar	4½oz (130g)	6½oz (185g)	8oz (225g)
Self-raising flour	4½oz (130g)	6½oz (185g)	8oz (225g)
Plain flour	2½oz (60g)	3oz (90g)	4½oz (130g)
Eggs (large)	2	3	4
Cooking time (hours)	¾–1	1–1¼	1¼–1½

See page 156 for recipe method

Round 8in (20cm) Square 7in (18cm)	Round 9in (23cm) Square 8in (20cm)	Round 10in (25cm) Square 9in (23cm)	Round 11in (28cm) Square 10in (25cm)
1lb 7oz (650g)	1lb 12oz (795g)	2lb 10oz (1.1kg)	3lb 5oz (1.5kg)
4oz (115g)	5oz (140g)	7oz (200g)	9oz (255g)
8 tablespoons	4fl oz (110ml)	5floz (140ml)	6fl oz (170ml)
1	1½	2	2
6oz (170g)	8oz (225g)	11oz (310g)	14oz (400g)
5oz (140g)	7oz (200g)	10oz (285g)	13oz (370g)
½ teaspoon	½ teaspoon	¾ teaspoon	¾ teaspoon
6½oz (185g)	8oz (225g)	12oz (340g)	1lb (455g)
¼ teaspoon	¼ teaspoon	½ teaspoon	½ teaspoon
¼ teaspoon	½ teaspoon	¾ teaspoon	¾ teaspoon
½ teaspoon	1 teaspoon	1 teaspoon	1 teaspoon
4	5	7	8
3 teaspoons	1 tablespoon	1½ tablespoons	1½ tablespoons
3½–4	4–4½	5–5½	About 6

See page 156 for recipe method

Round 8in (20cm) Square 7in (18cm)	Round 9in (23cm) Square 8in (20cm)	Round 10in (25cm) Square 9in (23cm)
6½oz (185g)	8oz (225g)	10oz (290g)
6½oz (185g)	8oz (225g)	10oz (290g)
12oz (360g)	1lb (455g)	1lb 2oz (510g)
12oz (360g)	1lb (455g)	1lb 2oz (510g)
6½oz (185g)	8oz (225g)	9oz (260g)
6	8	9
1–1½	1½–1¾	1½–2 hours

Fruit cake instructions

DAY BEFORE

1 Place all the dried fruits, rum or sherry and rind in a saucepan. Warm and stir over a low heat for a few minutes. Pour all the contents into a large bowl and allow to soak overnight.

NEXT DAY

2 Preheat the oven to 275°F/140°C/Gas mark 1.5 and prepare and line the cake tins.

3 Cream the butter and sugar together in a large bowl until pale and fluffy. Now sift the dry ingredients together.

4 Add the eggs, one at a time, alternating with tablespoons of the flour mixture to prevent the mixture curdling. Beat in the treacle.

5 Fold in the remaining dry ingredients and soaked fruit and mix well.

6 Place the mixture into the prepared tin.

7 Bake in a central position in the oven, or if using several shelves, rotate halfway through the cooking process.

8 Cook until a skewer inserted into the centre of the cake comes out cleanly. Allow to cool in the tin.

9 When cool, baste with the desired alcohol, then overwrap in fresh greaseproof paper and foil. Keep to mature, basting occasionally with the desired alcohol. Do NOT store in plastic boxes.

Madeira cake instructions

1 Preheat the oven to 325°F/160°C/Gas mark 3 and line the cake tin. Sift the flour.

2 Cream the butter or margarine and sugar together in a large bowl.

3 Add the egg and flour alternately to the creamed butter mixture, finishing with the flour.

4 Spoon the cake mixture into the prepared tin and bake in the oven until a skewer inserted into the centre of the cake comes out clean.

5 Allow to cool.

CHOCOLATE CAKE

To convert the recipe into a rich chocolate cake:

1 Substitute half the caster sugar with soft brown sugar.

2 Substitute ½oz (15g) of plain flour for ½oz (15g) of cocoa powder per egg in the recipe.

156

Filling cream or buttercream

You will need

- 4oz (115g) unsalted butter or margarine
- 13oz (375g) icing sugar (confectioner's sugar)
- 2 tablespoons water
- 2–4 tablespoons of unsweetened cocoa powder for chocolate buttercream

1 Beat the butter or margarine until it is light and fluffy.

2 Gradually add the water and icing sugar (on a slow speed if using an electric mixer).

3 Increase the speed of the mixer and continue to beat until the mixture becomes paler and is light enough in consistency to spread easily.

CHOCOLATE BUTTERCREAM

Add 2–4 tablespoons of unsweetened cocoa powder to the water before it is added to the mixture.

Royal icing

Royal icing is used for piping grass and hair, as well as adding extra detail, such as rows of little piped balls of icing on the White Sparkles cake (page 58). It is also great for fixing the decorations to your cake.

You will need

Makes about 8oz (225g)
- 1 egg white
- 1 teaspoon glycerine
- 8–9oz (225–250g) icing sugar, sifted

1 Put the egg white and glycerine into a bowl and beat in the icing sugar, a little at a time, until the icing is smooth, white and forms soft peaks when the spoon is pulled out.

2 Cover the bowl with a damp cloth and allow to stand for five minutes to disperse any air bubbles before use.

3 You can store the icing in an airtight container in a cool place, such as a refrigerator, for about ten days. It must be stirred thoroughly before use to bind together all the ingredients once again. If you do not stir thoroughly it will be difficult to work with and will not give a smooth finish.

Apricot purée and sugar glue

APRICOT PURÉE

Use apricot purée or sugar glue to stick pieces of icing together. Apricot purée is suitable for sticking large pieces and sugar glue for smaller pieces.

You will need
Makes 5fl oz (150ml)
- 5½oz (150g) apricot jam
- 2–3 tablespoons water

1 Put the jam and water into a saucepan and heat gently, stirring occasionally, until the jam melts. (It can also be heated in a microwave oven.)

2 Rub through a sieve and allow to cool before using.

SUGAR GLUE

Sugar glue is an invaluable aid when fixing figures and small pieces of cake.

You will need
- ½oz (15g) simple pastillage
- 3 teaspoons cool boiled water

1 Break up the pastillage icing in a bowl and pour the water on top. Allow to soak for at least 30 minutes, then mix thoroughly to a thick paste.

2 Sugar glue can be used as soon as it is made. It will keep in an airtight container in the refrigerator for up to ten days.

Pastillage

Pastillage is a sugar-based dough used for making decorations, such as flowers (see 'Little Mouse', page 22). You can buy pastillage from cake suppliers but it is very easy to make your own.

You will need
Makes about 12oz (350g)
- 1 egg white
- 2 teaspoons gum tragacanth
- 12oz (350g) icing sugar, sifted

1 Put the egg white into a mixing bowl. Using 10oz (275g) of the sifted sugar, add to the egg white a little at a time, beating well to make a stiff consistency like royal icing. Level the top and sprinkle the gum tragacanth evenly over the surface. Allow to stand for ten minutes.

2 Turn the pastillage out on a work surface and knead together, incorporating the remaining icing sugar.

3 Lastly, wrap in a polythene bag and store in an airtight container.

Ready-made sugarpaste

This is sometimes referred to as 'fondant' or 'rollout' icing. It is easily bought in sugarcraft shops and supermarkets. It is available in white and many different colours. Using ready-coloured paste can save a lot of time, especially with darker colours such as red, green or black. White and coloured Regalice has been used throughout this book.

Colouring sugarpaste and royal icing

If you cannot buy readymade sugarpaste in the colour you require, buy white sugarpaste and colour it yourself. Use paste colours for best results, as they are more concentrated and give deeper, richer colours. Colour royal icing with paste colours too.

HOW TO COLOUR SUGARPASTE

1 Make a hole with your thumb in the middle of the piece of paste to be coloured. Dip a cocktail stick or toothpick into your chosen colour and then put the colour into the hole.

2 Fold the paste over and start to knead the colour in, using icing sugar to prevent it sticking to the work surface or to your hands. Add more colour as necessary to achieve the colour you require, but take care not to add too much.

TIP: *If you wish to colour your own sugarpaste icing, use paste colours in preference to powder or liquid colours. Powder colours can create a grainy effect and liquid colours can change the consistency of your sugarpaste and make it sticky.*

Making sugarpaste or fondant icing

You can buy ready-made sugarpaste or fondant icing from cake suppliers, but you can easily make your own.

You will need

Makes about 1lb 8oz (675g)
- 1 egg white
- 2 tablespoons liquid glucose
- 1lb 8oz (675g) icing sugar, sifted
- A little white fat (optional)

1 Put the egg white and liquid glucose into a bowl and gradually add the icing sugar. Stir until the mixture thickens.

2 Turn out on to a work surface dusted with icing sugar and knead until the paste is smooth and silky. If the paste becomes a little dry and cracked, try kneading in a little white fat.

Applying the sugarpaste to your prepared cake

1 Roll out your sugarpaste to a thickness of ⅛–⅙in (3–4 mm) on a surface dusted with icing sugar. Bring your cake as near to the rolled-out icing as possible, wrap your icing over your rolling pin and gently place it on your cake.

2 Gently smooth the icing around the top edge of your cake using the palms of your hands.

3 Work your way smoothly down the sides of your cake until you reach the base.

4 Use a smoother in circular motions to gently 'polish' the top of the cake. This will flatten the top and create a sheen on the surface of your icing.

5 Now, using small cuts, trim the icing off around the bottom of your cake.

6 Use the smoother around the sides of your cake to create beautifully straight sides.

7 Your cake is now ready to finish. To cover the silver board edge, follow the next three steps.

8 Brush on a very thin layer of water or apricot glaze. Roll out a strip of sugarpaste, cut a straight edge one side and wrap it around the silver board, add additional strips until all the board is covered.

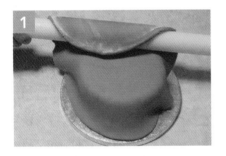

9 Trim all around the edge with little cuts, wipe your knife frequently and continue until the icing is trimmed all the way round.

10 Smooth around the icing on the board, especially over the joins.

Dowelling a cake

If you wish to place your cakes on top of each other, always dowel the lower tiers to prevent the top ones sinking down.

1 Push a piece of plastic dowelling into the cake until it reaches the cake drum. Mark a tiny scratch on the dowelling with a knife at the top surface of the cake, remove the dowelling, cut it with a saw knife at the mark, snap the piece off then replace it into the cake.

2 Now add two more pieces of dowelling for a round cake – place them in a triangular formation. Add three more pieces of dowelling for a square cake; place them in a square formation. Ensure that none of the pieces are higher than the surface of the cake, as this will prevent the top tier from resting level.

How to frill sugarpaste

You will need

- Garrett frill cutter or oval cutter
- Bulbous cone modelling tool

1 Cut out your circle with a garrett frill cutter or oval cutter. It should be about ⅛in (3mm) thick on a surface dusted with a LOT of icing sugar.

2 Bring your frill to the edge of your smooth flat work surface and roll the fattest part of the modelling tool along the very edge of your frill.

3 Start the next roll along your frill very slightly overlapping the previous one. Continue until you have rolled and frilled all the way around your circle or oval.

4 If you are using a garrett frill cutter, remove the round centre now and cut in half ready to stick on your cake.

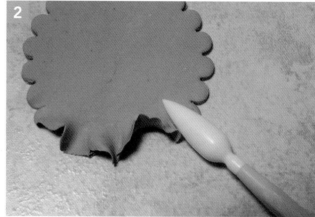

Making sugarpaste models

If you are a beginner, practise making a duck and a teddy before you make one of the more complicated models. Always use the Guide to Sizes chart, below, for all your animals and people, as this will save you having to guess the size of each body part.

Each time you create a part of your model, roll it into a smooth ball in the palm of your hands. The warmth of your hands will soften the paste and remove any lines or cracks from its surface. Now match the ball to the correct size ball on the chart. When it fits you are ready to start forming the required shape.

GUIDE TO SIZES CHART

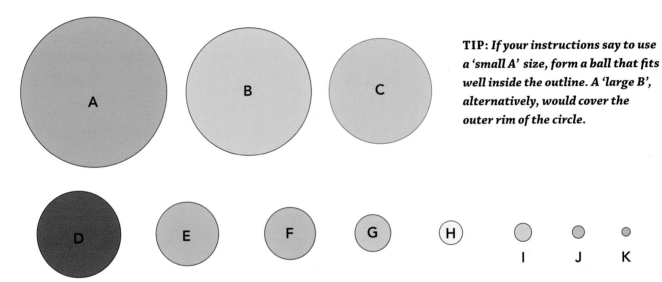

TIP: *If your instructions say to use a 'small A' size, form a ball that fits well inside the outline. A 'large B', alternatively, would cover the outer rim of the circle.*

HEADS

1 A baby's head is a round shape; fine hair can be scratched on with a cocktail stick or toothpick.

2 An adult's head is an oval shape (see 'Clown' and 'Soccer player', page 169.)

3 A lady's or little girl's head has a gently pointed chin, so that she will look more delicate (see 'Fairy', page 169.)

EYES

You will need
- Cocktail stick or toothpick
- Liquorice black paste colour

Dip the end of your cocktail stick into liquorice black paste colour.

Mark oval or long eyes – rest the black tip of the cocktail stick against the face to mark the eyes, and approach the head at the angle shown in the picture, to ensure that your eyes are long in preference to round dots.

Compare the two faces below
The one with long eyes (right) is much more friendly and appealing than the one with dot eyes (left).

TIP: *Do not mark the eyes as dots. Never push a cocktail stick into the front of the face, as this will form a little round eye and your model will look mean or unfriendly.*

SMILE OR A MOUTH

1 You can paint a smile on your face with a very fine paintbrush and black paste colour slightly diluted with painting solution.

2 You can give your little model an open mouth by pushing in a pointed tool.

Making a piping bag

1 Cut a piece of greaseproof or silicone paper into a long triangle with one corner cut off. If you are right-handed have this corner on your right, and the left if you are left-handed.

2 Pick up the right-hand corner and twist it inwards until a tight point is formed in the middle of the long side.

3 Rotate your hand inside until you have rolled to the end of the triangle and your cone is complete.

4 Bend the point of the paper inwards and tuck firmly into the cone.

5 Make a little rip halfway along, then fold over and bend one side inwards – this will secure the bag and stop it unravelling when you let go of it.

6 Fill the bottom half of your bag with peaky royal icing if you are piping hair or grass.

7 If you are adding a piping tube, rip the bottom ½in (1cm) off your bag, place the tube inside, then half-fill with royal icing.

8 Fold the open end of the bag over several times to secure the icing inside.

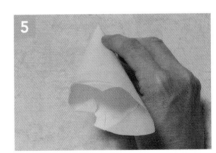

Piping

1 Half fill your bag with your coloured royal icing.

2 Pinch the pointed end flat between your fingers.

3 Cut the flat end as illustrated on the right with two snips.

4 Ensure that both cuts are the same length.

You are now ready to pipe grass or hair, as described below and on the facing page.

GRASS

1 Gently squeeze a blob of icing out of the bag, stop squeezing and pull the bag away; you will have formed a little spike.

2 To pipe long grass, continue to squeeze up the side of the cake and only pull away sharply having stopped squeezing when your blade of grass is the correct length.

CLOWN'S HAIR

By piping four or five little spikes each side of the white head in orange royal icing you will quickly complete the clown's hair.

FOOTBALLER'S HAIR

The hair of the footballer is made with lots of little spikes at the sides and really long spiky hair at the top of the head.

FAIRY'S HAIR

1 Start the fairy's hair at the top of the chin and pipe a long strand of icing upward, ending near the top of the head.

2 Repeat this action all the way around the back of the head to the other side of the face.

3 Add a little short fringe – if the icing is spiky on top allow to dry for a few minutes, then pat the spikes gently down to remove.

Cutter shapes

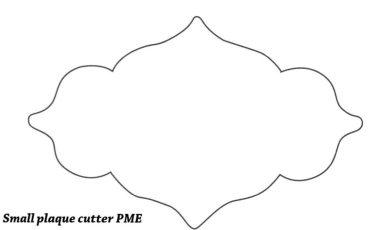

Small plaque cutter PME

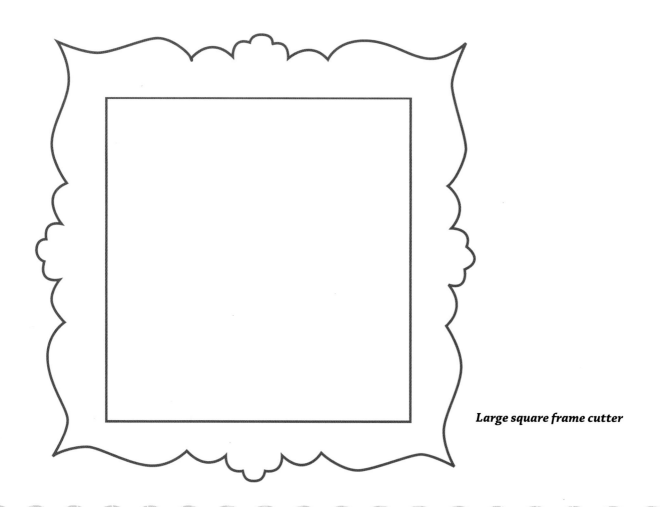

Large square frame cutter

Large round frame cutter

Jem doily plaque cutter

Templates

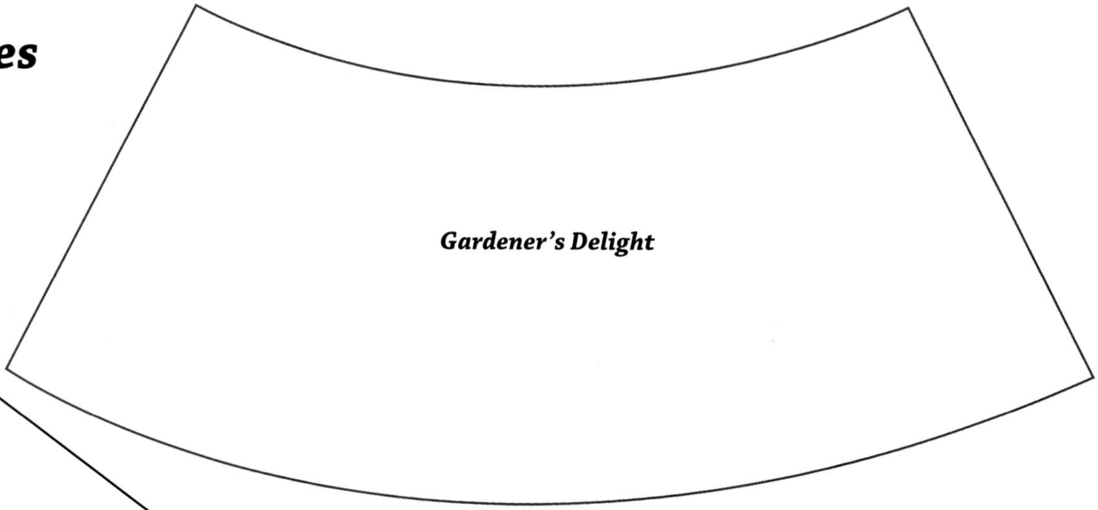

Gardener's Delight

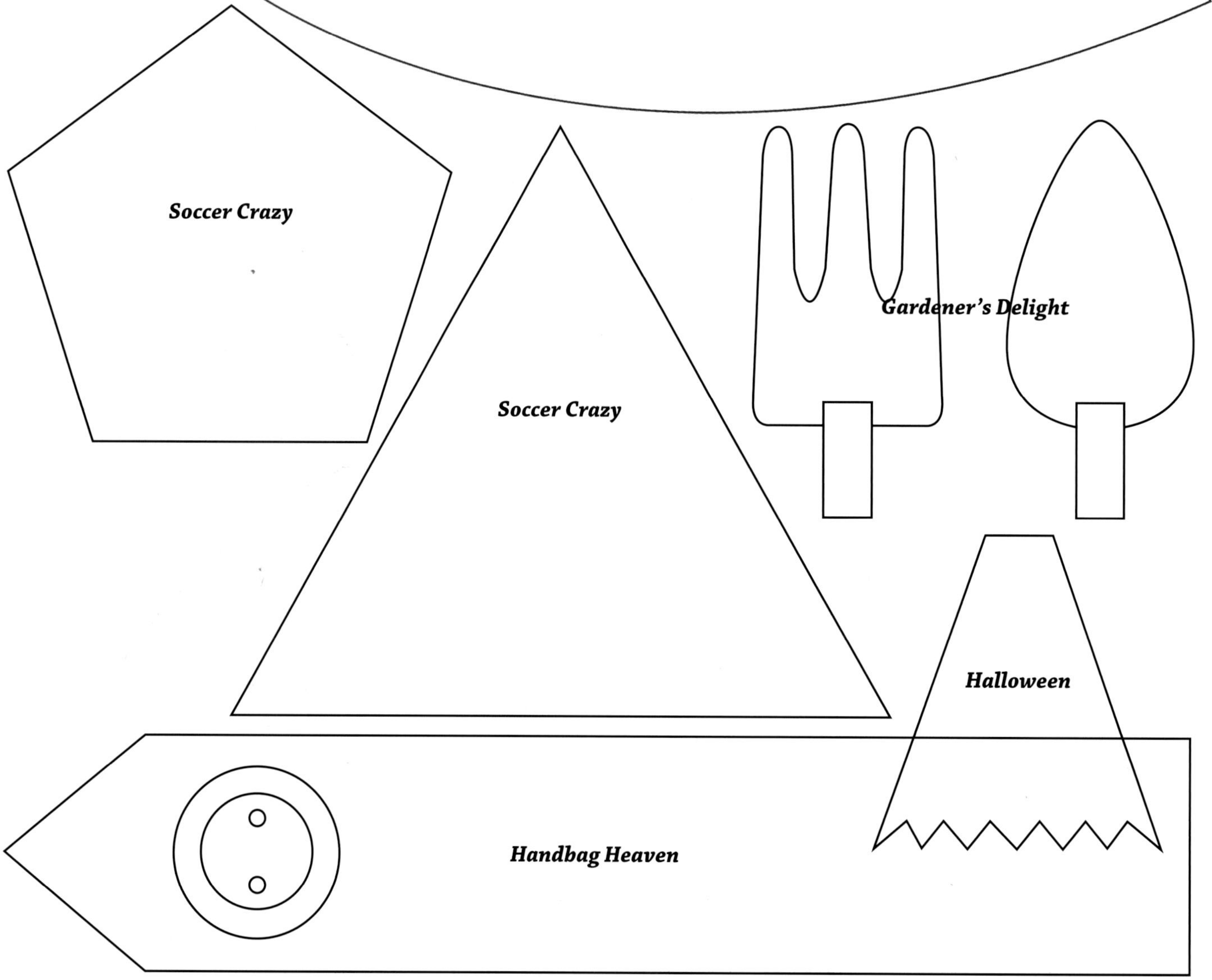

Soccer Crazy

Soccer Crazy

Gardener's Delight

Halloween

Handbag Heaven

172

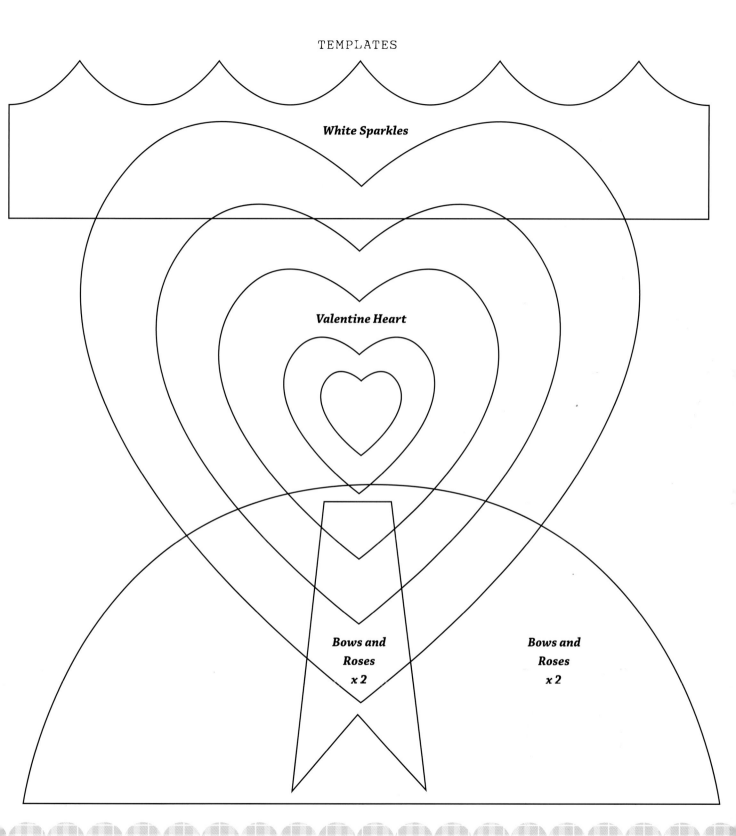

White Sparkles

Valentine Heart

Bows and
Roses
x 2

Bows and
Roses
x 2

Suppliers

UK

Ann Pickard
The Icing Centre
26 Nithsdale Road
Weston Super Mare, BS23 4JR
Tel: +44 (0)1934 624565
www.icingcentre.co.uk

COVA PASTE: white sugarpaste
BFP Wholesale Ltd
Unit 8 Connections
Industrial Centre
Vestry Road
Sevenoaks
TN14 5DF
www.bfpwholesale.com

Culpitt Ltd
Jubilee Industrial Estate
Ashington
Northumberland, NE63 8UQ
Tel: +44 (0)1670 814545
www.culpitt.com

Edable Art (EA)
1 Slanhope Close
The Grange
Spennymoor
Co Durham, DL16 6LZ

Fine Cut Sugarcraft (FC)
Workshop 4
Old Stable Block
Holme Pierrepont
Nottingham, N912 2LD
Tel: +44 (0)115 9334349
www.finecutsugarcraft.com

FMM Sugarcraft (FMM)
Unit 5
Kings Park Industrial Estate
Primrose Hill
Kings Langley
Hertfordshire, WD4 8ST
Tel: +44 (0)1923 268699
www.fmmsugarcraft.com

Guy Paul and Co Ltd
Unit 10, The Business Centre
Corinium Industrial Estate
Raans Road
Amersham
Bucks, HP6 6FB
Tel: +44 (0)1494 432121
www.guypaul.co.uk

Holly Products (HP)
Holly Cottage
Hassal Green
Sandbach
Cheshire, CW11 4YA
Tel: +44 (0)1270 761403
www.hollyproducts.co.uk

ICECRAFT: white sugarpaste
British Sugar plc
Sugar Way
Peterborough
PE2 9AY
Tel: +44 (0)1733 563171
www.britishsugar.co.uk

Lindy's Cake Ltd (LC)
17 Greville Avenue
Wendover
Bucks, HP22 6AG
Tel: +44 (0)1296 623906
www.lindyscakes.co.uk

Patchwork Cutters (PM)
3 Raines Close
Greasby
Wirral
Merseyside, CH49 2QB
Tel: +44 (0)151 6785053
www.patchworkcutters.co.uk

Knightsbridge PME
Unit 21 Riverwalk Road
(Off Jeffreys Road)
Enfield
EN3 7QN
Tel: +44 (0)20 3234 0049
www.cakedecoration.co.uk

REGALICE: white and coloured
sugarpaste
Renshawnapier
Crown Street
Liverpool
L8 7RF
Tel: +44 (0)151 706 8200
www.renshawnapier.co.uk

USA
Beryl's Cake Decorating & Pastry Supplies
PO Box 1584
North Springfield, VA 22151
Tel: 1-800-488-2749
www.beryls.com

Sugarcraft TM
3665 Dixie Hwy
Hamilton, OH 45015
www.sugarcraft.com

AUSTRALIA
Bakery Sugarcraft
198 Newton Road
Wetherill Park
NSW 2164
Tel: (02) 9676 2032
www.bakerysugarcraft.com.au

About the author

Ann Pickard qualified as a baker and cake decorator in 1983 and opened her shop, 'The Icing Centre', in 1986. She runs a successful cake-decorating business in Weston-super-Mare in Somerset, England, and has published eight books on cake decorating, including *Cake Characters* by GMC Publications. She has also produced a range of DVDs on the same subject.

Acknowledgements

Many thanks to:
Renshawnapier for supplying the Regalice sugarpaste for this book;
PME and Holly Products;
Janet Ostle – sugar flowers – Gardener's Delight;
Culpitts – sugar flowers – Draped Cascade.

BW 6/11

Index

To place an order, or to request a catalogue, contact:
GMC Publications
Castle Place, 166 High Street, Lewes, East Sussex, BN7 1XU
United Kingdom
Tel: +44 (0)1273 488005 Fax: +44 (0)1273 402866
Website: www.gmcbooks.com
Orders by credit card are accepted